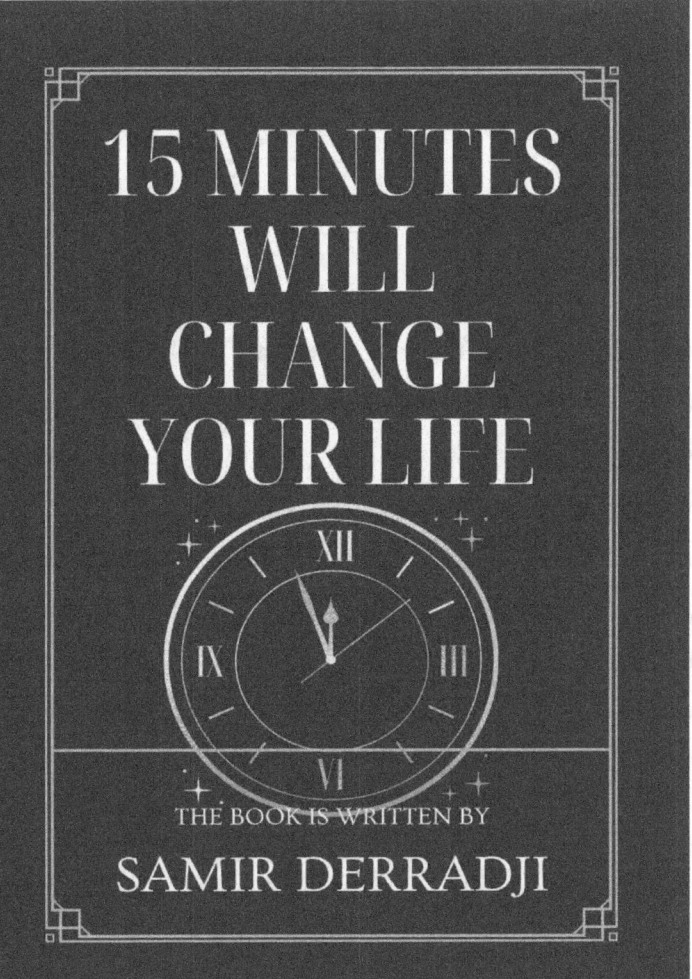

15 minutes change your life

introduction :

In today's world, time is our most valuable asset, but it's also our most wasteful. We make big and small financial decisions every day, but have you ever thought about how a little knowledge and investment in yourself can change the course of your entire life in just a few minutes? In this book, I'll introduce you to 15 minutes of concepts and tips that if applied wisely, will find yourself moving towards a more stable and prosperous financial life.

In just a few minutes, you'll learn how to manage your money, invest wisely, and put yourself on the right path to financial freedom. It may seem like 15 minutes is short, but it can make a big difference if you invest it correctly.

In this book, you will not find complexities or exaggerated advice. All you need is a few minutes a day, and you will start seeing tangible results.

1. **Section One: The Right Financial Mindset**
2. **Section Two: Managing Money Wisely**
3. **Section Three: Smart Investment**
4. **Section Four: Savings and Financial Hedging**
5. **Section Five: Overcoming Debt**
6. **Section Six: Financial Freedom**
7. **Section Seven: 15 Minutes a Day for Financial Change**

Section One: The Right Financial Mindset

The importance of positive financial thinking:

Positive financial thinking is one of the most important skills a person must acquire on their journey to financial success. Just as thoughts have a significant impact on a person's emotional and social life, they also have a direct impact on how an individual manages their money and makes wise financial decisions. In this section, we will discuss how positive financial thinking can impact your life, and what steps you can take to adopt this type of thinking to achieve financial freedom and prosperity.

1. Positive Financial Thinking: The Foundation for Financial Success

Positive financial thinking simply means viewing money as a tool to help you achieve your goals, not as a burden or a source of anxiety. People with a positive money mindset see opportunities everywhere and believe that they can achieve financial success through good planning and hard work. They don't view money as a problem, but rather as a means to enable them to live comfortably, meet their obligations, and achieve their dreams.

The financial success mindset begins with the belief that financial growth and personal progress are possible for everyone. People who embrace this mindset do not focus on lack of resources, but are always looking for ways to increase their income and improve their financial situation.

2. How does negative financial thinking affect your life?

Conversely, negative financial thinking can be a major obstacle to financial success. When a person focuses on the fear of failure or sees money as scarce and difficult to obtain, they begin to make ill-considered financial decisions based on anxiety rather than wise planning. People with this mindset may become discouraged by large expenses or financial challenges, which causes them to avoid taking risks and not look for opportunities that could improve their financial lives.

Over time, negative financial thinking can lead to poor financial habits such as not saving or failing to invest. Instead of seeing failure as an opportunity to learn, people with a negative mindset may stop trying altogether, leading to long-term financial stagnation.

3. Benefits of positive financial thinking

There are many benefits to positive financial thinking, which can completely transform your life:

1-**Confidence in making financial decisions:** When you believe that you are capable of achieving financial success, you become more willing to make bold and informed financial decisions. You will start looking for investment and personal development opportunities, instead of fearing failure.

2-**Increase income:** Positive thinking drives you to look for new ways to improve your income. Whether it's developing your skills or starting a side project, you'll feel motivated to achieve more financial success.

3-**Overcoming financial crises:** Positive-minded people view financial crises as opportunities to learn and grow. Instead of feeling hopeless, they start looking for solutions and rely on their creativity to improve their situation.

4-**Personal growth:** Positive thinking makes you a more resilient and stronger person. When you believe in your ability to achieve financial success, you become more willing to develop yourself and face challenges with patience and determination.

4. Steps to Adopting Positive Financial Thinking

If you want to change your mindset towards money, here are some steps you can take:

1-**Focus on opportunities, not obstacles:** Instead of dwelling on what you don't have, focus on the opportunities you do have. Look for ways to improve your income, whether it's through hard work, investing, or developing your personal skills.

2-**Set clear financial goals:** Positive thinking begins with setting clear, achievable goals. Whether you want to buy a home, start a business, or achieve financial freedom, setting a specific goal helps you create a plan to achieve it.

3-Use positivity in talking to yourself: Stop using negative phrases like "I can't" or "I won't succeed." Instead, use positive phrases that boost your self-confidence like "I am capable of achieving financial success" and "I can manage my money wisely."

4-Learn from your financial mistakes: Instead of getting discouraged by financial mistakes, view them as opportunities to learn and grow. Ask yourself: What can I learn from this? How can I improve my future decisions?

5-Build positive financial habits: Positive thinking alone is not enough. There must be actions that translate this thinking into daily habits such as regular saving, thoughtful investing, and setting a monthly budget.

6-Find inspiration: Read financial success stories of people who started from scratch and achieved great success. These stories inspire you and remind you that financial success is available to anyone who is willing to work hard and adopt a success mindset.

5. The impact of the surrounding environment on financial thinking

The environment we live in has a huge impact on how we think about money. If you're surrounded by people who are negative or unwilling to improve their financial lives, you may feel discouraged or reluctant to adopt a success mindset. Conversely, if you're surrounded by people who support and motivate you to improve your financial situation, you'll be more willing to take bold steps and achieve financial success.

Therefore, it is important to surround yourself with positive people who push you forward. Find partners who share your financial vision and ambition, and learn from people who have successfully achieved their financial goals.

6. The long-term impact of positive financial thinking

Shifting to a positive financial mindset doesn't happen overnight, but it takes time and effort. However, the results you achieve will be tangible and long-lasting. Over time, you will start to notice a significant improvement in the way you manage your money, and you will be able to achieve financial goals that you thought were out of reach.

Conclusion: Adopting a Financial Success Mindset

Positive financial thinking is not just a slogan or a passing thought, it is the foundation for achieving financial success. When you start adopting this type of thinking, you will notice a change in the way you deal with money and make financial decisions. You will become more confident in your ability to achieve success, and more prepared to overcome the financial challenges that may face you.

How do you start changing your financial habits?

Changing your financial habits is an essential step to achieving financial stability and prosperity. Many people find themselves stuck in unhealthy financial patterns such as overspending, not being able to save, or even failing to plan for future spending. But the good news is that these habits can be changed with simple, sustainable steps. If you want to improve your financial situation and adopt new habits that will help you reach your goals, here is a practical guide to get you started.

1. Awareness of current financial situation

The first step to changing your financial habits is to understand your current financial situation. Without this understanding, it will be difficult to know where to start. Follow these steps :

- **Fixed Income Definition:** Calculate the total monthly income you receive, whether from work, side projects, or any additional sources of income.

- **Expense analysis:** Write down all your monthly expenses, from rent and bills to small everyday expenses like food and entertainment. This analysis will give you a clear idea of where you might be spending unnecessary money.

- **Determine debts and obligations:** Make sure you know what debts you have, whether they are bank loans, credit cards, or even personal debts.

Once you have this clear visualization, you will be able to start identifying the habits that need to be changed.

2. Setting financial goals

Setting financial goals is an essential step towards improving your financial habits. Habits cannot be changed without a clear vision of what you want to achieve. Make sure your financial goals are specific and achievable. For example:

- **Short-term goals:** Such as saving up for a new phone or taking a short vacation.

- **Medium-term goals:** Such as saving a down payment for a car or apartment.

- **Long term goals:** Such as saving for retirement or building a sustainable investment.

These goals provide you with the motivation to keep working on improving your financial habits.

3. Develop a financial budget

Budgeting is the most effective tool for improving financial habits. Creating a budget allows you to control spending, saving, and achieving your goals. Simple steps can help you build an effective budget:

- **Planning monthly spending:** Allocate a specific amount for each spending category (rent, food, entertainment, savings).

- **Adherence to correct financial ratios:** For example, try not to spend more on housing than 30% of your monthly income, and try to allocate 20% of the income to savings.

- **Monthly evaluation:** Review your budget regularly to make sure you're on track. If you're having trouble sticking to it, make adjustments as needed.

Budgeting makes you more aware of your daily expenses and helps you discover opportunities where you can improve your financial situation.

4. Break the cycle of unnecessary spending

One of the biggest negative financial habits is unnecessary spending. You may find yourself spending on things you don't really need, either out of habit or a momentary urge. To change this habit:

- **Think before you buy:** Ask yourself: Is this something necessary? Can I wait before making a decision? This thinking can limit impulsive buying.

- **Use a shopping list:** When you go shopping, whether for groceries or other purchases, make sure to write down a list of what you need and stick to it.

- **Emotional spending analysis:** Sometimes spending is triggered by emotions like sadness or anxiety. Try to identify when this happens and replace the habit with other, non-financial activities like exercise or reading.

5. Develop a saving habit

Saving is one of the basic financial habits you need to adopt if you want to improve your financial situation. Some simple steps can help you build this habit:

- **Save first:** Before you start spending, set aside a portion of your income for savings, whether it's 10% or 20%. You can set up an automatic transfer from your checking account to your savings account to ensure compliance.

- **Setting savings goals:** Having a specific savings goal, such as building an emergency fund or saving for travel, helps you stay committed to your plan.

- **Avoid using savings unjustifiably:** Be careful not to use the saved money on unnecessary expenses. Try to keep this money for the goals you have set.

6. Invest in yourself

In addition to changing your daily financial habits, it is also important to invest in yourself to develop your financial skills and abilities. This includes :

- **Financial learning:** Always try to develop your financial knowledge by reading books, following economic blogs, or attending educational courses on how to manage money and invest.

- **Professional development:** Investing in improving your professional skills can increase your income and improve your career opportunities, which can enhance your overall financial situation.

- **Thinking about the future:** In addition to saving, consider investing part of your money in projects or markets that will provide you with long-term returns, such as real estate or stocks.

-

7. Commitment to continuous change

Changing your financial habits doesn't happen overnight. It takes consistent commitment and patience. It's important to understand that financial success comes over time, and real change requires small but sustainable steps. Try to evaluate your financial habits regularly and make sure you're moving in the right direction.

Periodic evaluation: Review your financial achievements periodically. Are you making progress towards your goals? Are there any habits that need to be modified?

Flexibility: If you encounter challenges or mistakes, don't give up. Use these opportunities to learn and grow. Adapting to financial changes will be part of your habit improvement journey.

8. Positive impact of the surrounding environment

The environment around you has a huge impact on how your financial habits are shaped. Surround yourself with people who encourage you to succeed financially, and stay away from people who push you to spend irresponsibly or spread negativity.

- **Find a supportive community:** Find friends or groups online who share your financial vision, where you can exchange tips and experiences.

- **Learn from the experts:** Follow the success stories of people who have managed to improve their financial lives. These people can be a source of inspiration and motivation.

Conclusion: Adopting healthy financial habits

Changing your financial habits takes awareness, planning, and long-term commitment. By being aware of your current financial situation, setting goals, developing a budget, and changing negative patterns, you can build strong financial habits that will enable you to achieve financial success and live freely and prosperously. Remember, change comes with time and practice, and every small step you take toward improving your habits will bring you closer to your financial goals.

"If you don't discover the secret behind the paragraphs after reading them, either reread them with greater concentration, or close the book and go to sleep."

.

Turning financial goals into actionable plans

Setting financial goals is an important step in the journey to financial success, but without turning those goals into clear, actionable plans, they may remain just unattainable dreams. Turning financial goals into actionable plans is a process that requires systematic thinking, good planning, and discipline in execution. In this section, we will explore how to turn your financial goals into concrete, actionable, and follow-through plans.

1. Clearly define financial goals.

The first step toward turning financial goals into actionable plans is to make sure your goals are clear and specific. If your goals are vague or unmeasurable, they will be difficult to achieve. Here's how to set clear financial goals:

- **Use the formSMART** This model is a global standard for setting goals, where they should be:

- **Specific (Specific):** Your goal should be clear and specific. Instead of saying, "I want to save," state, "I want to save an amount."$15,000 at the end of the year."

- **Measurable (Measurable):** You should be able to track your progress toward your goal. Determine how you will measure progress, such as setting a specific amount to save each month.

- **Achievable Achievable):** Make sure the goal is realistic and achievable based on your current income and ability to save.

- **Related (Relevant):** The goal should be related to your financial needs and priorities. Don't choose a goal just because it sounds attractive, but because it serves your long-term financial plan.

- **time-boundTime-bound):** Set a time frame for achieving the goal. For example, "I want to save $100,000."$10,000 at the end of 12 months."

Once you set your goals according to this model, you will have taken a big step towards making them actionable.

2. Analysis of the current financial situation

Before you can start making practical plans, you need to know clearly where to start. This requires a comprehensive review of your current financial situation. Here's how to do it:

- **Income and expense analysis:** Calculate all the sources of income you receive on a monthly or annual basis. Then identify the fixed monthly expenses (such as rent and bills) and variable expenses (such as entertainment and food).

- **Identify debts and financial obligations:** Review all the debts you need to pay off (loans, credit cards, etc.), and determine the interest you pay on these debts.

- **Review of financial assets:** Check the financial assets you have such as savings, investments, property, etc. These assets can be part of your financial plan to help you achieve your goals.

Analyzing your current financial situation is a crucial step because it gives you an accurate view of your available resources and the obligations you need to take into account when making your plan.

3. Break big goals into small steps.

Big financial goals like buying a house or saving for retirement can often be daunting and difficult to achieve at first. But breaking them down into smaller steps can make them easier and more manageable. Here's how to break down goals:

- **Monthly or weekly plans:** Set small steps that you can take on a regular basis. For example, if your goal is to save $100,000,$10,000 in one year, divide the amount by 12 months or 52 weeks to determine how much you need to save in each period.

- **Focus on priorities:** You may have multiple financial goals, so it's important to prioritize them. Start with the most urgent goals or those that can have the biggest impact on your financial life.

- **Identify the necessary resources:** If the goal requires an investment or purchase of specific assets, be sure to identify the financial resources you need and how to obtain them.

Breaking it down into small steps makes the goal seem more achievable and gives you a sense of accomplishment with each small step you take.

4. Create a financial budget that matches the goals.

A budget is the practical tool that turns goals into reality. Without a good budget, it will be difficult to control spending and achieve goals. Here's how to create a budget that supports your goals:

- **Allocate a portion of income to each goal:** After reviewing your monthly income and identifying your essential expenses, allocate a specific portion of your income to achieve your financial goals. This amount can be part of your monthly savings or a regular investment.

- **Control expenses:** Try to cut down on unnecessary expenses to save more money to achieve your goals. For example, you can cut down on entertainment or online shopping.

- **Automatic saving:** Using the automatic transfer feature from your checking account to a savings account can help you achieve your savings goals without having to think about them every month.

Creating a balanced financial budget can make achieving your financial goals more organized and easier to follow.

5. Invest wisely to achieve long-term goals.

For long-term financial goals like retirement or buying a home, saving alone may not be enough. That's where investing comes in as part of your financial plan. Here are some tips for investing wisely:

- **Understanding Risk and Reward:** Before you invest, make sure you understand the risks associated with each type of investment. Stocks, real estate, or bonds have different levels of risk and return.

- **Diversification:** It is important to diversify your investment portfolio. Do not put all your money in one type of investment, but spread it across different markets to reduce risk.

- **Long-term investment:** For long-term goals, it is better to choose investments that will provide long-term returns. Stocks, for example, may be volatile in the short term, but tend to grow over the long term.

Investing can be an effective way to achieve big goals that may take years to achieve.

6. Periodic follow-up and modification when necessary.

Turning goals into actionable plans is not a static process, but rather one that must be reviewed and adjusted over time. Changing economic conditions, increased income, or even changes in priorities can affect your financial plans. Here's how to follow through effectively:

- **Review plans periodically:** Review your financial plan at least once every three months. Are you making progress toward your goals? Do you need to adjust your budget?

- **Benefit from financial instruments:** Use financial apps or software to track your spending and savings.

These tools help give you a clear picture of your progress.

- **Adapting to changes:** Your financial circumstances may change over time, whether with increased income or unexpected expenses. Be flexible in adjusting your plan so that it remains in line with your current financial situation.

Regular follow-up helps ensure you are on the right track and allows for adjustments to be made when necessary.

7. Commitment and patience to achieve financial goals

Commitment and patience are key to achieving financial goals. Big goals like buying a home or retiring early often take a long time to achieve. It's important to stay committed to your plan, even if things move slowly at first.

- **Celebrating small successes:** Whenever you achieve part of a goal, celebrate it. This helps motivate you to keep going.

- **Stay away from frustration:** If you encounter obstacles or delays in achieving your goals, don't get discouraged. Use these obstacles as opportunities to learn and adapt.

Commitment to a structured financial plan is what separates those who achieve their goals from those who give up halfway through.

Conclusion: From Goals to Practical Implementation

Turning financial goals into actionable plans is a process that requires careful planning, patience, and commitment. By setting clear goals, breaking them down into small steps, and creating an effective budget, you can make your financial dreams a reality. Remember, progress may be slow at first, but with consistent follow-through and commitment, you will be able to achieve goals that you thought were out of reach.

2. Section Two: Managing Money Wisely

Before I start talking about the other topic, I would like to share a short story about my friend and I when we were young. My friend worked in a factory, and the working conditions there were very bad. The place was dirty and dusty, and the machines were old, so much so that you could sometimes see rats. In addition, the owner of the factory was operating illegally. However, my friend did not stop working there, he worked at night.

When I asked him, "Why don't you stop working there?", he always said that he was getting paid well, and I could attest to that; he was getting paid more than I was. At the time, I was working in a grocery store. The work wasn't stressful, and the place was clean, but I wasn't making much money. I saved everything I made, though, because I didn't want to work all day for someone else. My friend spent most of his earnings on unhealthy food, expensive clothes, and useless things.

When I advised him to stop this pattern, he always told me that the money he earned was not enough to do anything useful with it, and even if he saved it, he would not be able to achieve anything. My friend was very negative, and had negative thoughts about saving.

Over time, with the money I saved, I was able to start my own business. I no longer needed to work for anyone every day, but I could study, play sports, and participate in other activities. I could also travel whenever I wanted. My friend, who had negative thoughts and was not good at saving, never developed. He is still working.8 hours a day, and spends everything he earns before the end of the month.

The moral of the story is the importance of financial planning and wise management of resources to achieve success and stability in life. The story highlights several key points:

- **Saving and investing for the future**Focusing on saving and investing money wisely can lead to financial freedom and enable a person to build their future. While enjoying money immediately without planning prevents achieving big goals.

- **The effect of positive and negative thoughts** Positive thoughts about money and saving promote success and progress, while negative thoughts hinder development and keep a person stuck in the same situation.

- **Short-term sacrifice for long-term gain** Giving up some pleasures and extra spending today can provide bigger and better opportunities in the future.

- **Independence and control of life** By saving and planning, a person can become financially independent and have more flexibility in their life, allowing them to achieve other goals such as traveling or developing their skills.

Overall, the story teaches us that smart financial decisions and long-term thinking are the key to achieving success and stability in life.

Identifying sources of income and how to enhance them

In today's world, diversifying your income streams is vital to achieving financial stability and increasing economic opportunities. Relying on just one source of income can make you vulnerable to economic fluctuations or changes in the job market. Therefore, it is important to understand your current sources of income and work to enhance them or add new ones. In this article, we will discuss how to identify different sources of income and how to enhance them to achieve financial stability and growth.

1. Identify current sources of income

The first step in building a strategy to boost your income is to identify the sources of income you currently rely on. These sources may be multiple or limited to one income, but it is important to identify all of them to analyze their ability to meet your financial needs. The following are the most prominent types of income sources:

- **Income from primary job:** This is the most common source of income for most people. It is your monthly or weekly salary from your current job. Whether you work full-time or part-time, your steady income from your job is a major source of money.

- **Side business income:** You can have side projects that you work on outside of work hours, such as freelancing (Freelancing), providing consulting services, or selling products online. These businesses help supplement your primary income.

- **Income from investments:** If you own investments, whether in stocks, bonds or real estate, these investments may provide you with periodic financial returns. These returns can be a source of additional income that is fixed or fluctuating depending on the type of investment.

- **Rental income:** If you own one or more properties, renting them out can be a sustainable source of income. Rental income depends on demand in the real estate market but can be a steady source of income over the long term.

- **Income from self-employmentFreelancing):**Freelancing is one of the most popular sources of additional income. You can offer services in your field such as design, programming, writing, or any other skill you have, and get paid based on the projects you complete.

2. How to enhance existing income sources

After identifying your sources of income, the next step is to work on enhancing them or improving the financial returns you get from each source. This requires taking practical steps to improve your financial situation. Here are some ways to enhance your income:

- **Increase your salary in the main job:**

- **Salary negotiation:** If you feel that your current salary does not match the amount of work you do or the qualifications you possess, it may be time to negotiate a salary increase. Start by analyzing the value of what you bring to the company, then request a meeting with your manager to discuss the matter professionally.

- **Professional development:** Invest in yourself by developing your skills or obtaining recognized certifications in your field. Improving your professional skills can increase your value in the job market, making it easier to advance in your career and increase your salary.

- **Increase income from side businesses:**

  - **Expanding the scope of work:** If you offer services such as freelancing or consulting, try to expand the scope of clients you deal with. Use online freelancing platforms to reach a wider audience.

  - **Improve your services or products:** Improve the quality of the products or services you offer.

The better your services, the more likely customers will pay higher prices. You may also consider adding new services or different packages to cater to a wider range of customers.

- **Focus on marketing:** Using social media and digital marketing can help you attract more clients to your side business. Create a website or blog to showcase your business and get attention.

- **Increase returns on investments:**

  - **Re-evaluate your investment portfolio:** Review your investments regularly to make sure they are working for you. If you have investments that are not generating the desired returns, it may be time to rebalance your portfolio. Diversified investments can help you achieve stable growth.

  - **Investing in new assets:** If you want to boost your investment income, consider adding new types of assets such as real estate or investments in index funds (ETFs) that provide long-term returns.

- **Increase income from real estate and rentals:**
    - **Improve rental properties:** If you own rental property, making improvements to it such as upgrading utilities or providing additional services may allow you to increase the rent. Also, if you have extra space in your home, you can rent it out for additional income.
    - **Investing in new properties:** If you have the financial ability, buying new properties and renting them out can increase your cash flow. Try to invest in areas with high rental demand to improve your profit opportunities.

3. Add new sources of income

In addition to enhancing your current income streams, it's important to consider adding new ones. Diversifying your income reduces financial risk and increases your chances for financial growth. Here are some ideas for adding new income streams:

- **Starting a business:** If you have an innovative business idea, it may be time to start a business.

Whether online or in the real world, businesses offer the opportunity to generate significant income in the long run.

- **Investing in education and skills:** Learning new skills can open new doors for you in the job market or can enable you to offer new services or products. For example, learning programming or digital marketing may allow you to offer services that are in high demand.

- **Benefit from the Internet:** The Internet offers endless opportunities to make money. You can start a blog, YouTube channel, or social media account and generate income through advertising or affiliate marketing. You can also sell digital products like e-books or courses.

4. Continuous follow-up and development

Increasing and improving your income doesn't happen overnight. You must be willing to track your income and evaluate your performance regularly. Make sure to be flexible and willing to change your strategies when needed. Continuously developing your professional skills and investments can be the difference in boosting your income streams.

Conclusion

Diversifying and increasing your income streams is a vital strategy for achieving financial security and independence. By identifying your current income streams, increasing them, and adding new ones, you can build a strong financial foundation that will allow you to meet financial challenges and achieve your goals.

Secrets of controlling daily expenses

Controlling daily expenses is one of the essential keys to successfully managing finances and achieving long-term financial security. Many people find themselves in difficult financial situations due to unorganized or random spending, so learning how to control daily expenses is a necessary step towards improving your financial situation and achieving future goals. In this article, we will discuss the most important secrets and practical tips that can help you manage daily expenses effectively.

1. Prepare a daily and monthly budget

The first and most important step to controlling your daily expenses is to create a budget. This financial plan helps you track your expenses and see where your money is being spent on a daily basis, making it easier for you to identify areas where you can save. Here's how to create a budget:

- **Determine your monthly income accurately:** Your budget should be based on your net income, that is, after taxes, insurance, and any other obligations have been deducted. This way, you know how much you can actually control.

- **Divide expenses into categories:** Break down your expenses into specific categories such as food, transportation, bills, entertainment, and shopping. This will help you understand exactly where your money is going and reveal categories where you can cut back.

- **Allocate a daily budget:** Based on your monthly expenses, you can set a specific daily amount that allows you to spend without exceeding the limits. For example, if your budget for food and entertainment is $300 per month, you can allocate $10 per day for these two purposes.

2. Monitor expenses regularly.

After setting up a budget, it is essential that you monitor your expenses on a regular basis. This process allows you to understand your consumption patterns and identify opportunities for savings. Here are some effective methods for monitoring expenses:

Use of financial applications: There are many apps available that help you record your expenses and compare them to your budget. For example, you can use apps like Mint or YNAB to record every purchase and manage money smartly.

Keep receipts: Keep all purchase receipts for a period of time, and review them regularly to identify excess or unnecessary spending.

Weekly review: Set aside time each week to review your expenses and compare them to your budget. This gives you the opportunity to correct mistakes before they accumulate and negatively impact your financial situation.

3. Reduce unnecessary expenses

One of the most important secrets to controlling daily expenses is the ability to distinguish between necessary expenses and unnecessary ones. Unnecessary expenses are those that can be eliminated or reduced without significantly affecting your lifestyle. Here are some tips to reduce these expenses:

Give up expensive habits: If you're used to buying coffee or eating out on a daily basis, it might be time to cut back on this type of spending. Prepare your meals at home or make your own coffee and you'll notice the difference at the end of the month.

Avoid impulse buying: Try to avoid emotional or unplanned shopping. Before you buy something, ask yourself if you really need the product or if you can postpone buying it.

Use of coupons and offers: Try to take advantage of special offers and coupons to save money when shopping. This may seem like a small savings, but it can add up in the long run and help you cut your spending significantly.

4. Plan your spending in advance.

Planning your daily spending in advance can help you avoid a lot of extra expenses. Having a plan in advance for each day or week can help you focus on priorities and avoid unnecessary expenses. Here's how to plan your spending:

Preparing a shopping list: Before you go shopping, make a list of all the things you need and stick to it. This prevents you from getting carried away with buying unnecessary things.

Setting financial priorities: Break your expenses down into essential expenses (such as bills and necessities) and leisure expenses (such as entertainment and personal shopping). Prioritize essential expenses and make sure they are covered first before considering any leisure expenses.

Meal planning: Preparing a weekly meal plan can help save you money and time. Instead of spending on takeout or restaurants, prepare your meals in advance based on your food budget.

5. Invest in high-quality goods.

Sometimes, buying cheaper items may seem like a better option to save money, but it can actually lead to higher expenses in the long run. Buying higher quality items that last longer can be a wise investment that helps reduce spending in the long run. Here are some examples:

- **Clothing and shoes:** Instead of buying cheap clothes or shoes that will wear out quickly, invest in high-quality products that will last for years. The initial purchase cost may be higher, but you will save money in the long run.

- **Home appliances:** When it comes to electronic or home appliances, it is always better to invest in a reliable brand with high quality, as it will serve you longer and require less maintenance.

6. Avoid financial traps

There are some financial traps that you may fall into without realizing it and lead to overspending. It is important to be aware of these traps and avoid them to stay committed to your budget. The most prominent of these traps are:

Fake promotions: Some deals may seem tempting, like "buy one, get one half price," but they can make you buy things you don't really need. Make sure the deals you take advantage of are tailored to your real needs.

Online shopping: Online shopping can be easy and tempting because of the constant offers and discounts. Make sure to set limits on your online shopping and don't get carried away by the discounts unless you really need what you're buying.

Credit cards: Over-reliance on credit cards can cause you to spend more than you should. Try using cash or debit cards to avoid the high interest rates that come with credit cards.

7. Automatic saving

One of the best-kept secrets to controlling your daily expenses is automatic savings. Instead of relying on your willpower to save money, you can set up an automatic savings system that takes a portion of your income and directs it directly into a savings account. Here's how to do it:

- **Create a separate savings account:** Open a bank account specifically for savings, and do not use this account for daily expenses. This will help you focus on the main goal of saving.

- **Set a fixed amount to save each month:** Decide on a specific amount you want to save each month and program your bank account to automatically transfer this amount at the beginning of each month to your savings account.

8. Find cheaper alternatives

In every aspect of daily life, you can always look for cheaper alternatives that allow you to reduce expenses without significantly compromising on quality. For example:

- **Food:** Instead of eating out, you can prepare meals at home. Also, buying products in bulk can help you save money.

- **Transportation:** Try to use public transportation instead of a private car or paid services such as taxis or apps.

- **Entertainment:** Look for free or low-cost recreational activities such as taking a walk in the park or attending free events in your city.

Conclusion

Controlling your daily expenses isn't difficult if you're willing to take a few simple steps and stick to a budget. By planning well, monitoring your expenses, and avoiding financial traps, you can achieve financial security and dramatically improve your quality of life. Using these practical secrets will help you manage your money more wisely and put you on the right path to achieving your financial goals.

How to Build an Effective Budget That Fits Your Needs

Creating an effective budget is an essential step to successful financial management and financial stability. Whether you're trying to meet specific savings goals, get out of debt, or just looking to manage your money more organized, a budget is a vital tool to ensure you stay on top of your spending and income. In this article, we'll cover how to create an effective budget that fits your needs and helps you achieve your financial goals.

1. Determine your financial goals

The first step in creating an effective budget is to define your financial goals. It's important to know what you're trying to achieve with your money management. Are you trying to save money to buy a house? Get rid of credit card debt? Or do you want to build an emergency fund? Here are some examples of financial goals that can help guide your budgeting:

- **Short-term goals:** Such as buying a new electronic device or saving for a short trip. These goals are usually achievable over a period of time ranging from a few months to a year.

- **Medium-term goals:** Such as buying a car or paying off student loans. These goals take between one and five years to achieve.

- **Long-term goals:** Such as buying a home or retiring early. These goals may take several years or even decades to achieve.

Clearly defining goals helps you prioritize and focus on what matters to you in your financial plan.

2. Analyze your monthly income

Once you have your goals in place, it's important to know exactly how much money comes into your account each month. This includes your primary income from your job or freelance work, as well as any additional sources of income such as returns from investments or rent. It's important to calculate your net income, which is after taxes, insurance, and any other deductions have been taken out.

If your income is irregular, such as if you are a freelancer, try to estimate your average monthly income based on previous months. This helps you create a more realistic budget that fits your financial situation.

3. Identify fixed and variable expenses

The next step in building an effective budget is to analyze your monthly expenses. Expenses can be divided into two basic types: fixed and variable expenses.

- **Fixed expenses:** These are expenses that don't change much from month to month and include rent, bills (electricity, water, internet), monthly payments, and subscriptions (such as gym memberships or streaming services). These expenses are usually necessary and can't be easily reduced.

- **Variable expenses:** It includes everything that changes depending on your needs and consumption habits, such as food expenses, entertainment, transportation, shopping, etc. These expenses can be more controlled by making wise choices.

To better organize your budget, record these expenses in a table and analyze them in depth to identify any unnecessary or inefficient expenses.

4. Follow the 50/30/20 rule to divide the budget.

There are many ways to divide a budget, but the rule is:50/30/20 is one of the most popular and effective methods. Under this rule, your monthly income is divided into three main categories:

- **50% for basic expenses:** This category includes all basic expenses that cannot be avoided such as rent, bills, and necessary expenses such as food and transportation.

- **30% for entertainment expenses:** This category includes entertainment or non-essential expenses such as going out to eat, personal shopping, or travel.

The goal here is to keep these expenses to no more than 30% of your income.

- **20% for savings or debt repayment:** This category is set aside for saving or investing toward your long-term financial goals, such as building an emergency fund or paying off debt. If you're looking to get out of debt, you can allocate a larger portion of this category toward paying off debt faster.

5. Review regular bills and expenses.

An important step in building an effective budget is to review your regular bills and see if you can reduce them. For example, you can:

- **Negotiating invoices:** You may be able to negotiate with service providers such as internet or electricity to get better deals or lower-cost plans.

- **Reduce subscriptions:** If you subscribe to multiple services like streaming platforms or gyms, it might be wise to review these subscriptions and see if you're actually using them. If you're not using some of them regularly, it might be best to cancel or put them on hold.

6. Reduce variable expenses

Variable expenses are usually the part of your budget that you can control. Reducing these expenses can help you increase your savings or pay off debt faster. Here are some tips to reduce variable expenses:

- **Preparing meals at home:** Instead of eating out frequently, try preparing your meals at home. This can significantly reduce your food expenses.

- **Relying on public transportation:** If you can use public transportation instead of a car, it can save a lot of money on fuel and maintenance.

- **Planning your shopping:** Make a shopping list before you go shopping and stick to it. Avoid impulse buying that leads to unnecessary expenses.

7. Prepare an emergency fund

An important part of any budget is to set aside a percentage of your income to create an emergency fund. This fund can help you deal with unexpected expenses like medical bills or car repairs. It's best to have enough of an emergency fund to cover your basic expenses for a period of 3 to 6 months.

If you don't have an emergency fund yet, you can start with a small amount each month and direct a portion of your savings to this fund until it becomes strong enough.

8. Continuous follow-up and modification when needed.

Building an effective budget is not a static thing, but rather requires ongoing monitoring and adjustments when needed. It is essential that you review your budget monthly to determine whether you are on track or not. Here are some points to consider during the review:

- **Expense analysis:** Review recurring expenses and make sure they do not exceed the limits you have set in your budget.

- **Achieving goals:** Make sure you're meeting the savings or debt repayment goals you set at the beginning of your budget.

- **Budget adjustment:** If you notice that some expenses frequently exceed expectations, you may need to reallocate some categories in the budget or cut back on unnecessary expenses.

9. Use of financial tools and applications

To manage your budget more effectively, you can take advantage of financial apps that help you track your expenses and set up your budget easily. There are many apps such as "Mint or YNAB, which provide tools for tracking income and expenses, and provide monthly reports that help you accurately understand your financial situation.

Conclusion

Building an effective budget that fits your needs takes some planning and organization, but it's not an impossible task. By setting your financial goals, analyzing your income and expenses, and using strategies like the 50/30/20, you can create a budget that will help you achieve financial stability and achieve your goals. Consistency and constant follow-up are the keys to ensuring the success of the budget and achieving tangible results.

3. Section Three: Smart Investment

Investing Basics: Where to Start?

Investing is an effective way to build wealth and achieve long-term financial stability. Whether you are looking to secure your retirement or simply supplement your current income, investing provides an opportunity to grow your capital over time. But many beginners find it difficult to know where to start, especially with so many options available. In this article, we will review the basics of investing and how you can start your investment journey with confidence and success.

1. Understand the basics of investing

Before you start investing your money, it is important to understand what investing means. Simply put, investing is the process of purchasing assets (such as stocks, real estate, or bonds) with the goal of generating future returns. Returns vary depending on the type of investment and your risk tolerance, so it is important to be fully aware of the following basic concepts:

- **Return (Return):** It is the profit or loss resulting from your investment. The return can be in the form of income (such as dividends) or an increase in the value of the asset itself (such as an increase in the price of a stock).

- **riskRisk):** Every investment carries a certain degree of risk, which is the possibility of losing some or all of the money invested. The higher the risk, the higher the potential return, and vice versa.

- **Portfolio diversification Diversification):** A basic principle of investing is to spread your money across several assets or investment types to reduce risk. Diversification means you don't put all your eggs in one basket, which protects you from unexpected market fluctuations.

2. Determine your financial goals

Before you start any investment, you should define your financial goals. Do you want to save for retirement? Are you planning to buy a home or finance your children's education? Setting goals helps you choose the right type of investment and the time frame you need to achieve these goals.

- **Short-term goals:** These goals can be of less than 5 years, such as saving for a trip or buying a car. In this case, you may prefer more stable, lower-risk investments such as bonds or savings accounts.

- **Long-term goals:** Goals that take more than 10 years to achieve, such as planning for retirement. In this case, you may want to consider riskier investments such as stocks or real estate, as they have a higher potential for significant returns in the long run.

3. Assess your risk tolerance

Everyone has a different risk tolerance. Risk tolerance depends on several factors, including age, financial goals, and overall financial situation. If you are early in your career, you may be able to take higher risks because you have enough time to recoup any potential losses. If you are nearing retirement, you may want to invest in less risky investments to preserve your capital.

You can assess your risk tolerance by answering some personal questions:

- How would you feel if the value of your investments fell by 20% in a short period?

- Do you need cash in the near future?

- Do you prefer investments with fixed returns but less risk?

Based on your answers, you can choose investments that match your risk tolerance.

4. Choosing the right type of investment

Once you have determined your financial goals and risk tolerance, you must decide which type of investment is right for you. There are many options available, each with its own advantages and disadvantages:

- **Stocks (Stocks):** Stocks represent an ownership stake in a particular company. Stocks may provide high returns over the long term, but they come with high risks, as stock prices can fluctuate greatly.

- **Bonds (Bonds):** Bonds are loans made to corporations or governments in exchange for a fixed interest. They are less risky investments than stocks, but they offer lower returns.

- **Mutual fundsMutual Funds):** These funds pool investors' money to invest in a variety of stocks or bonds. Mutual funds provide easy diversification and are managed by professional financial institutions.

- **Real estate (Real Estate):** Buying real estate can be a long-term investment that provides steady rental income or increases in property value over time.

- **Digital currencies (Cryptocurrency):** Cryptocurrencies like Bitcoin are newer and high-risk investments. They can yield great returns but require deep research and understanding of the market.

5. Start small and invest continuously

A common mistake beginners make is thinking they need a large amount of money to start investing. The reality is that many investments can be started with very small amounts. You can start with a small amount and gradually increase it over time. The most important thing is to be consistent with your investments and stick to a long-term plan.

- **Regular investment strategy:** One of the best ways to invest regularly is to use the dollar-cost averaging strategy.Dollar-Cost Averaging). This strategy involves investing a fixed amount at regular times (e.g. monthly) regardless of market conditions. This means you will buy more assets when prices are low and less when prices are high, reducing the impact of volatility.

6. Continuing financial education

Investing is not just buying assets and waiting for them to grow. You need to be prepared to learn more about the market and keep up with economic developments. Financial education helps you make better investment decisions and reduce risks. You can take advantage of financial books, blogs, and podcasts to learn more about the world of investing.

Some popular books that may help you on your journey:

- "The Intelligent Investor" by Benjamin Graham
- Rich Dad Poor Dad by Robert Kiyosaki
- ""The Little Book of Common Sense Investing" by John Bogle

7. Consult a financial advisor

If you're still not sure where to start, it may be a good idea to consult a professional financial advisor. A financial advisor can help you define your goals, assess your risk tolerance, and guide you toward investments that are right for you. Of course, it's important to choose a reliable and licensed advisor.

8. Start investing gradually.

There is no need to invest all your money at once. You can start with small amounts and gradually increase them as you gain experience and confidence in the market. This method helps you learn from mistakes and reduce the risks associated with investing.

9. Monitoring and evaluating investments

After you start investing, it is essential to regularly monitor the performance of your investments and evaluate how well they are meeting your financial goals. Use the financial tools and reports available to monitor the performance of your investment portfolio and make adjustments if necessary. Some points to consider include:

- **Performance review:** Compare the returns on your investments with the goals you set and with the general market performance.

- **Rebalancing:** Over time, the asset allocation ratios in your investment portfolio may change due to market fluctuations. Rebalance your portfolio regularly to ensure you continue to achieve your financial goals.

- **Continuous learning:** Stay informed of the latest economic and financial developments, and continue learning about new investment strategies to improve your financial performance.

9. Deal with risks intelligently

Investing involves risk, but this risk can be managed intelligently by:

- **Diversification of investments:** As mentioned earlier, diversifying an investment portfolio reduces risk and increases the chances of achieving stable returns.

- **Determine the appropriate level of risk:** Choose the types of investments that match your risk tolerance and financial goals.

- **Holding investments for the long term:** Reducing frequent trading and focusing on long-term investments can help you weather market volatility and achieve better returns.

10. Hire a financial advisor

If you are unsure about how to start investing or need help building an appropriate investment strategy, it may be helpful to consult a professional financial advisor. A financial advisor can provide personalized advice based on your financial situation and goals, and help you make informed investment decisions.

Conclusion

Investing is a long journey that requires patience and planning. By understanding the basics of investing, defining your goals, and assessing your risk tolerance, you can begin to build a strong and stable financial future. Remember, success in investing does not come overnight, but rather depends on commitment, discipline, and perseverance over the long term.

Investing in assets: gold, real estate, stocks

Investing in assets is one of the most popular ways to grow wealth over the long term. Among these assets, gold, real estate, and stocks are the most prominent options that attract the attention of investors. Each of these assets has unique characteristics in terms of risk and return, and has its own secrets that make it a special choice for some people. In this article, we will learn the essential details of each of gold, real estate, and stocks, in addition to how to get the most out of them as an investor.

Gold: A Safe Investment in Times of Crisis

Gold has been considered a safe haven for investors for thousands of years, especially in times of financial and economic crises. Among the most important reasons that attract investors to gold are:

1- Protection from inflation: Gold is a physical asset that retains its value even during times of inflation. When prices rise and currencies lose their purchasing power, gold remains stable or rises in value, making it an excellent hedge against inflation.

2- Stability in times of crisis: In times of political or economic turmoil, gold is seen as a safe haven. Many investors turn to gold when financial markets are turbulent, causing its price to increase.

3- Portfolio diversification: Because gold doesn't move the same way as stocks or bonds, it's an excellent option for diversifying a portfolio. Diversification reduces risk and increases the chances of consistent returns.

How to invest in gold

There are several ways you can invest in gold:

- **Buy physical gold:** This includes gold bullion and coins. Although owning physical gold provides investors with a tangible sense of security, storage and transportation can be expensive and require additional security measures.

- **Investing in gold exchange-traded funds (ETFs):** These funds provide investors with the opportunity to own gold without having to deal with the hassles of storage. Buying a share in a gold ETF is equivalent to buying a fraction of the gold itself.

- **Buying shares in gold mining companies:** Some investors may prefer to invest in companies that mine gold. Although this option offers higher returns if gold prices rise, it comes with additional risks associated with the performance of the company itself.

Secrets of investing in gold

- **Timing is everything.** Gold prices rise in times of crisis and fall with economic stability. Therefore, good timing when buying or selling gold can make a big difference in making big profits.

- **Don't rely entirely on gold.** Although gold is a safe haven asset, relying too heavily on it can deprive you of other investment opportunities. It is best to use gold as part of a comprehensive diversification strategy.

Real Estate: A Stable and Profitable Investment

Investing in real estate is one of the most stable and profitable options in the long term. The property has a real value that increases over time, and provides investors with the opportunity to benefit from a steady income from rentals or to make profits upon resale.

Why invest in real estate?

1- Stability: Real estate is generally considered less volatile than stocks or commodities. Even in economic crises, real estate prices may decline temporarily but often return to growth in the long run.

2- Generating a fixed income: If you own a property that you can rent out, it means you have a steady income every month. This income can be useful in achieving your financial stability or paying off property debt.

3-Direct control: Unlike stocks or bonds, investing in real estate gives you direct control over your assets. You can improve the property to increase its value, or change it as the market needs it.

Forms of real estate investment

- **Buying residential or commercial properties:** Buying property to rent or sell is one of the most popular forms of real estate investment. Residential or commercial properties offer investors the potential for significant long-term profits.

- **Real Estate Investment Trusts (REITs):** If you don't want to deal with the hassle of managing a property, you can invest in real estate investment trusts. These funds allow investors to invest in real estate without having to buy the property itself.

- **Land investment:** Undeveloped land can be a great investment opportunity. The value of the land can increase significantly over time, especially if it is located in an area that is promising for development.

Real Estate Investment Secrets

- **Location selection is key:** One of the most important secrets in real estate investing is location. Properties in good locations always yield better returns and retain their value. Make sure to study emerging areas and anticipate future developments.

- **Anticipate unexpected expenses:** In real estate investing, there are always unexpected costs such as maintenance or repairs. Make sure to allocate a portion of your budget for these expenses to ensure you don't run into financial trouble.

Stocks: High returns but with risks

Stocks represent an ownership stake in a particular company, meaning you become a partner in the success or failure of that company. Investing in stocks can provide great returns over the long term, but it comes with higher risks compared to gold or real estate.

Why invest in stocks?

1- Huge growth potential: Historically, stocks have delivered higher returns than most other investments over the long term. If you invest in successful companies, you can make big profits.

2- Liquidity: Stocks offer higher liquidity compared to real estate. You can buy or sell stocks quickly and easily without having to wait long.

3- Income from dividends: Some companies offer annual or quarterly dividends to shareholders, providing you with additional income on your investment.

How to invest in stocks

- **Direct investment in stocks:** You can buy individual stocks of companies that you believe will grow over the long term. However, you should be aware that your investment can be subject to market fluctuations.

- **Index funds (ETFs):** These funds allow you to invest in a wide range of stocks at one time, providing you with diversification and reduced risk.

- **International stocks:** Investing in international markets can provide new opportunities for diversification and higher returns.

Stock Investing Secrets

- **Don't try to time the market:** One of the most common secrets in stock investing is to avoid trying to time the market. It is very difficult to predict daily market movements, so long-term investing is most effective.

- **Research well before you buy:** Don't buy stocks based on rumors or quick tips. Make sure you study the company, its financial history, and its future growth strategies before making a decision.

Conclusion

Investing in the three assets: gold, real estate, and stocks, provides diverse opportunities to grow wealth and achieve financial stability. Each asset has its own characteristics and advantages, so it is important to diversify your investment portfolio to ensure the best returns while minimizing risks. Whether you are leaning towards stable investments such as real estate and gold, or looking for high growth potential with stocks, the real secret remains careful analysis and good, continuous planning.

The importance of diversification in the investment portfolio

Diversification is one of the key pillars of any successful investment strategy, and it plays a crucial role in reducing risk and increasing the chances of achieving good returns. Simply put, diversification means spreading your investments across several assets or sectors rather than focusing on one type of investment. This strategy, which some refer to as "don't put all your eggs in one basket," provides the investor with protection from market volatility and protects capital from large losses.

In this article, we will talk about the importance of diversification in an investment portfolio, the reasons for its success, and how to apply it effectively in your investments.

1. Reduce risks

One of the most significant benefits of diversification is risk reduction. When you invest in a variety of assets, you become less vulnerable to huge losses. The main reason for this is that different markets and assets do not usually move in the same direction at the same time. For example, while stock prices may fall during economic downturns, real estate or gold may remain stable or even rise.

How does diversification help reduce risk?

- **Geographical distribution:** Investing in global markets can reduce your dependence on the performance of a single domestic market. If you invest in global stocks, you may find that some international markets perform better during periods of domestic market downturns.

- **Diversification of assets:** Different assets such as stocks, bonds, gold, and real estate are not affected by economic factors in the same way. This means that spreading investments across multiple asset types can protect your portfolio from the risks associated with the volatility of any particular market.

- **Distribution to different sectors:** Diversifying across different economic sectors such as technology, health, energy, and finance provides protection from recessions that may affect one sector more than another.

2. Increase revenue opportunities

While the primary goal of diversification is to reduce risk, it can also increase your chances of achieving greater returns. When you invest in a variety of assets and markets, you increase your chances of taking advantage of positive trends in some markets or sectors that you may not have anticipated.

For example:

- Technology markets may experience rapid growth during a certain period, while other markets may stabilize. If you have invested part of your money in technology stocks, you will make good profits from this growth.

- At the same time, if you have investments in bonds or gold, you may benefit from their stability when financial markets are turbulent.

3. Protection from market fluctuations

Financial markets are notoriously volatile. Sometimes these fluctuations can be significant, and can result in significant losses if you focus on one type of asset. Diversification protects you from these fluctuations because it helps spread your risk across different assets. In other words, if one class of investments suffers losses, another class may be able to offset those losses.

- **Example:** During the financial crisis of the year 2008, global financial markets suffered a major collapse. However, investors who had diversified their assets across real estate, gold, and bonds were able to achieve relative stability in their financial portfolios.

4. Adapting to different economic cycles

Economies go through different economic cycles including recovery, growth, recession, and contraction. Each of these phases affects different types of investments. Stocks typically perform well during periods of growth, while gold and bonds tend to perform better during periods of recession or contraction. Therefore, by diversifying your portfolio, you ensure that you are prepared for any upcoming economic cycle, and not relying on just one type of asset.

5. Reducing the impact of wrong individual decisions

When you focus your investments on one type of asset or one sector, any mistake in choosing the right asset or company can lead to significant losses. Diversification reduces the impact of these types of mistakes, because even if one investment fails, others may be able to compensate for the losses.

6. Diversification and Psychological Risk Management

Investing is not only a financial process, it is also a psychological one. When you invest in one asset or one market, you may find yourself more concerned about the volatility and daily news associated with that asset. Diversification reduces this psychological stress because it allows you to rest assured that a portion of your investments is protected from direct market influences.

How to Effectively Apply Diversification in an Investment Portfolio

Now that you know the importance of diversification, let's look at how to put it into practice:

1- Diversification across different assets: Make sure you don't put all your money into stocks or bonds alone. Instead, try to spread your investments across a variety of assets such as real estate, gold, commodities, and stocks.

2- Geographical diversification: Don't limit your investments to one market or country. Invest in international markets to reduce your exposure to local risks.

3- Time diversification: Spreading your investments over different time periods can also help reduce the impact of daily fluctuations. This could mean investing regularly throughout the year rather than putting all your money into the market at once.

4-Investing in index funds (ETFs) or mutual funds: If you are new to investing or don't have the time to manage multiple investments, you can consider investing in index funds or mutual funds. These funds provide you with automatic diversification as they contain a variety of assets.

5-Review the portfolio regularly: Once you have created a diversified portfolio, it is important to review it periodically to ensure that it remains balanced. You may need to adjust your portfolio based on market performance or changes in your financial goals.

Conclusion

Diversification of your investment portfolio is a crucial strategy for long-term financial success. By spreading your investments across a variety of assets and markets, you can reduce risk, increase your chances of returns, and adapt to market fluctuations and economic cycles. Diversification is a powerful tool that helps investors achieve greater financial stability and protects them from the huge losses that can result from relying on one type of asset.

story :

In the year2008, the world was experiencing one of the worst financial crises in modern history, the global financial crisis that resulted from the collapse of the housing market in the United States and led to the deterioration of financial markets around the world. At that time, almost everyone was panicking. Corporate leaders, investors, and ordinary people, all felt that the future was uncertain. Prices collapsed, stocks lost their value dramatically, and many investors lost their money and confidence in the market.

But in the middle of this chaos was a man named John. John had a steady job and wasn't a big investor, but he believed in smart, long-term investing. John didn't have a huge fortune, but he had small savings that he had built up over the years. Although he wasn't a financial expert, he had read a lot about investing strategies and economics. When the crisis hit, instead of panicking like many others, John saw the collapse as an unexpected opportunity.

Getting Started: Understanding the Market and the Opportunity

John knew that economic crises, while causing great losses in the short term, could provide tremendous opportunities in the long term. He read about economic history and learned how the market usually bounced back after major crises. This recovery, while taking time, was always accompanied by an increase in the value of the assets that had depreciated during the crises.

At the height of the crisis, everyone was selling their stocks for fear of losing everything, but John followed a completely different strategy. He had learned from investment books, especially from books like Benjamin Graham's "The Intelligent Investor," that one of the secrets of successful investing was the ability to buy when prices were low due to general fear in the market.

Although he wasn't entirely sure how things would play out, John believed that many of the strong companies that had been under pressure during the crisis would bounce back once the economy stabilized. For this reason, he decided to start buying shares in those companies that he knew were strong but whose shares had collapsed due to the general market panic.

Regular and systematic investment

John did not invest all of his money at once. Instead, he decided to follow a strategy known as "price averaging."Dollar-Cost Averaging (DCA), a strategy that involves buying the same amount of stock on a regular basis regardless of the stock price. This strategy allows investors to profit from market fluctuations without trying to time the market, which many believe is impossible. Under this strategy, John would buy stocks when prices were low, and continue buying even if prices rose slightly.

Over time, John was able to accumulate a diverse portfolio of stocks in large companies such as Apple, Amazon, and Google. Although many of these companies were suffering from the repercussions of the crisis, John was confident that their fundamental strength would help them recover.

Patience is the key

Investing wasn't easy, it required a lot of patience and discipline. As the months went by, there was no immediate sign of improvement. The stocks John had bought continued to fluctuate, and the economic news was still very negative. Although John followed the market news daily, he stuck to his plan and didn't sell any of his stocks.

During this time, many of his friends and family began to question his decision. They saw that the market was still in a downturn, and there were rumors that things could get worse. However, John remained calm. He knew that patience is an essential part of any successful investment strategy, and that panic and haste often lead to poor financial decisions.

Recovery phase

Over time, the markets slowly began to improve. Some companies began to regain some of their market value, and confidence in the economy gradually began to return. John continued to invest regularly, even as prices began to rise, because he believed that the market had not yet reached its full potential. He knew that the market would take years to fully recover, but he was willing to wait.

During this period, John began reading more about the global economy and following growth trends in technology and e-commerce. He realized that innovation in technology would be the driving force for the coming decades, so he invested a larger portion of his savings in leading technology companies. Companies like Tesla and Microsoft were among the options he focused on.

reaping the fruits

After about ten years of investing, John's investments began to show results. The value of the stocks he bought at low prices during the crisis multiplied many times over. For example, Apple shares that he bought for less than$100 per share was worth many times that. Amazon and Tesla shares also rose dramatically, making his investment portfolio hugely profitable.

John didn't become a millionaire overnight, but he was able to build a significant amount of wealth sustainably through his careful investments and patience. Instead of panicking and pulling back during times of crisis, he took advantage and invested when everyone else was pulling back.

Lessons learned

From John's story, we can draw several valuable lessons that can help us make smart investment decisions:

1. **Long term investing is the path to success.** John wasn't looking for a quick profit, but rather he was committed to a long-term investment plan. This patience is what helped him achieve great returns over time.

2. **Taking advantage of crises**: Instead of panicking and dumping assets during crises, John saw the opportunity to buy at low prices. Crises can present great opportunities if you are prepared for them and understand the market well.

3. **Portfolio diversification** John didn't put all his money into one stock or one sector. Instead, he invested in a variety of companies, which helped him reduce risk and increase his chances of success.

4. **Knowledge is power** Reading and learning about economics and financial markets gave John the confidence to make informed decisions. He knew that markets go through cycles and that patience would eventually pay off.

5. **Adapting to changes** John's investments in technology companies such as: **Apple****Amazon** was a response to the great changes in the global economy. Innovation and technology were becoming the driving force of the economy, and John was ready to take advantage of this shift.

Conclusion

Ultimately, John's success was not the result of luck, but rather the product of careful planning, continuous education, and smart investing. The Financial Crisis of 20082008 was an opportunity, not a threat. He took advantage of it wisely and patiently, and over time he built a significant fortune. His story reminds us that smart investing is not about timing the market, but about sticking to a well-thought-out strategy and seizing opportunities when others walk away.

4. Section Four: Savings and Financial Hedging

Building an Emergency Fund: The Importance of Monthly Savings

Unexpected financial crises are an integral part of our daily lives, and they can occur at any moment, whether it is a job loss, health accidents, or unexpected emergency expenses. This is where the importance of an emergency fund comes in, which can be an ideal solution to face these emergency situations without falling into debt or financial stress. Building an emergency fund depends mainly on monthly savings, which is one of the basic strategies that can contribute to enhancing the financial security of individuals and families.

In this article, we will discuss the importance of monthly savings in building an emergency fund, talk about how to plan for it, and provide effective tips on how to build this fund in an effective and sustainable way.

First: What is an emergency fund?

An emergency fund is a sum of money set aside to cover unexpected and emergency expenses. This fund should be easily accessible in case of need, and it provides the investor or individual with the financial security that enables him or her to overcome financial crises flexibly and without resorting to borrowing or selling assets.

The most important thing about an emergency fund is that it should be used for emergencies only, such as job loss, unexpected medical expenses, or sudden car or home repairs. Therefore, it is not recommended to use it to cover regular expenses or luxury desires.

Second: The importance of monthly savings to build an emergency fund

1-Achieving financial security

Regular monthly savings are the surest path to financial security. When you commit to saving a set amount each month for an emergency fund, you gradually build a safety net that will help you weather unexpected financial crises. This financial security reduces the stress that can result from not being prepared for crises, and gives you a sense of control over your finances.

2- Avoid resorting to debts

One of the biggest risks people face in emergencies is resorting to loans or credit cards to cover expenses. Loans often come with high interest rates that increase financial burdens, while credit cards increase financial risks in the long run. Building an emergency fund through monthly savings helps you avoid these risks, as you can rely on your own savings to cover these expenses without the need for debt.

3-Providing protection for the family

If you have a family, building an emergency fund becomes even more important. Financial crises don't just affect the individual, they affect the entire family. Having an emergency fund ensures that you are able to provide for your family's basic needs in the event of a loss of income or an emergency expense.

4- Achieving long-term financial stability

Building an emergency fund through monthly savings is not just a temporary solution to crises, it is also an important step towards long-term financial stability. Once you have built a sufficient emergency fund, you can move towards achieving larger financial goals such as investing or early retirement. Saving monthly puts you on a steady path towards achieving these financial goals.

Third: How to build an emergency fund

1- Determine the amount required for the emergency fund.

Before you start saving, you should determine how much money you need for an emergency fund. It is generally recommended that you have an amount equivalent to 3 to 6 months of basic living expenses. This includes rent or mortgage, bills, food, and health expenses.

For example, if your monthly expenses are estimated at $2,000, the ideal emergency fund should be between $6,000 and $12,000.

2- Determine the monthly savings amount

Based on your monthly income and your ability to save, determine a reasonable amount that you can save each month. This amount could be 10% or 20% of your monthly income, or any other percentage that suits your financial situation. The goal is to commit to saving monthly without affecting basic expenses.

3- Use a separate savings account

To ensure that your emergency funds aren't used for everyday expenses, it's a good idea to open a separate savings account for your emergency fund. This allows you to track your savings progress and prevents you from accidentally spending the money.

4- Commitment to continuity

One of the most important factors in successful monthly saving is consistency. Committing to saving a set amount each month, no matter what, is what ensures that your emergency fund grows over time. You can use self-motivation techniques, such as setting small goals over short periods of time, to help you maintain consistency in saving.

Fourth: Tips to speed up building an emergency fund

1- Reduce unnecessary expenses

To increase your monthly savings and speed up the buildup of your emergency fund, it's important to review your monthly expenses and identify unnecessary expenses that can be reduced or eliminated. For example, you may be able to cut back on entertainment or eating out and transfer that money to an emergency fund.

2- Increase income

If monthly savings seem difficult with your current income, you may want to consider ways to supplement your income. These methods may include working part-time, starting a side business, or even leveraging your freelance skills. These additional sources of income can provide a huge boost to building an emergency fund more quickly.

3- Benefit from bonuses and allowances

If you get bonuses or raises at work, you can put a large portion of them into an emergency fund. This extra money can go a long way toward helping you reach your savings goal in a shorter time frame.

4- Use automatic saving

To avoid forgetting or delaying your monthly savings, you can set up an automatic savings feature. Many banks offer this service, where a set amount is transferred each month from your checking account to your emergency fund savings account. This method makes saving an automatic part of your financial routine..

Fifth: When should you use the emergency fund?

Once you have built an emergency fund, you should be careful about how you use it. This fund is only intended for true financial emergencies such as loss of income, unexpected medical expenses, or urgent home or car repairs. It should be avoided for everyday expenses or personal desires such as buying new appliances or taking recreational trips.

If you have to use your emergency fund, make sure to replenish it immediately after you use it. The goal is to maintain a certain level of money in the fund to ensure it is prepared for any future crisis.

Conclusion

Building an emergency fund through monthly savings is a necessary strategy for every individual seeking financial stability and security against sudden financial crises. By setting aside an appropriate amount for an emergency fund, committing to monthly savings, and reducing unnecessary expenses, you can build a financial safety net that gives you confidence and comfort in the face of unexpected challenges.

Different ways to protect yourself from financial crises

Financial crises can happen at any time and unexpectedly, whether it's due to a job loss, an economic downturn, or emergency medical expenses. No matter the nature of the crisis, preparing ahead of time and adopting sound financial strategies can help you better weather financial crises and maintain your financial stability. In this article, we'll cover a range of different ways to protect yourself from financial crises.

1. Build an emergency fund

One of the most effective ways to protect yourself from financial crises is to build an emergency fund. As discussed in previous topics, an emergency fund is an account set aside to cover unexpected expenses that may arise in an emergency such as job loss or sudden medical costs.

- **Emergency fund size:** It is best to have an emergency fund that contains enough money to cover living expenses for a period of between 3 to 6 months. This amount gives you enough time to manage your affairs and look for solutions without having to resort to debt.
- **How to build the box:** You can start by saving a small percentage of your monthly income, such as: 10% to 20%, until you reach the target amount.

2. Diversification of income sources

Relying on a single source of income can pose a significant risk to your financial stability, especially in the event of job loss or a decrease in your main income. One effective way to protect yourself from financial crises is to diversify your sources of income. This can be achieved by:

- **Freelancing or side projects:** You can use your personal skills to work on small projects or provide services online. Freelancing gives you more flexibility in earning money and provides an additional source of income that enhances your financial stability.

- **Investing in income-generating assets:** Such as buying real estate and renting it out or investing in dividend-paying stocks. These investments provide additional cash flow on a regular basis.

3. Avoid excessive debt.

Debt can be a double-edged sword. While loans may be necessary to achieve certain goals, such as buying a home or financing a project, excessive debt can lead to financial collapse in the event of a crisis. To reduce the impact of debt on your financial stability:

- **Get rid of high interest debt:** Your first goal should be to get rid of high-interest debt such as credit cards. These debts can quickly escalate if you can't pay them off, increasing your debt burden and making it harder to get through financial crises.

- **Limit borrowing:** Try to avoid unnecessary borrowing and only use debt in cases where you really need it and the interest is greater than the cost of borrowing.

4. Invest in your professional skills

Improving your professional skills increases your ability to adapt to changes in the job market and reduces the likelihood of losing your job. If you have advanced and in-demand skills, you will have a greater chance of getting new jobs in the event of a financial crisis. Ways to improve your skills include:

- **Continuous learning:** Stay up to date with the latest developments in your career field through educational courses or training programs. You can take advantage of online educational opportunities to develop your skills.

- **Diversify skills:** Don't limit yourself to just one skill. The more diverse your skills are, the more likely you are to find jobs or offer multiple services.

5. Investing in long-term assets

Investing in long-term assets such as real estate, stocks, or bonds can provide you with additional protection against financial crises. These assets typically increase in value over time, providing a steady cash flow that you can rely on in the event of a crisis. Some tips for investing wisely:

- **Diversify the investment portfolio:** Don't put all your money into one type of investment. Instead, diversify your portfolio across multiple markets and different assets, such as stocks, bonds, gold, and real estate.

- **Investing in assets with stable value:** Some assets, such as gold, tend to maintain or increase their value during economic crises. You can invest in these assets as part of your strategy to protect yourself from economic fluctuations.

6. Prepare an effective budget

Creating a monthly budget and sticking to it is a fundamental part of good financial management. A budget helps you monitor your expenses and ensure that you are not spending more than you earn. Steps you can take to improve your budget include:

- **Monthly Expense Analysis:** Review all monthly expenses and identify unnecessary expenses that can be reduced or eliminated.

- **Split income wisely:** Set aside a certain percentage of your income for saving and investing, another percentage for fixed expenses like bills, and another percentage for variable expenses like entertainment.

- **Monitor daily expenses:** Using financial apps or spreadsheets, you can monitor your daily spending and control unplanned expenses.

7. Health and life insurance

Health insurance and life insurance are vital tools to protect you from financial crises related to health or unexpected death. Unexpected medical costs can be a huge burden on your budget, so it is important to make sure you have health insurance that covers these costs.

- **health insurance:** It is important to choose health insurance that covers basic medical needs in addition to preventive checkups.

- **life insurance:** If you are responsible for supporting your family, having life insurance is a financial security for your family in the event of an unexpected death.

8. Maintaining liquidity

It is wise to keep a portion of your money in the form of cash that can be easily accessed in case of an emergency. Long-term investments may not be readily available during a crisis, so it is important to keep enough cash in a savings or checking account that can be used in an emergency.

- **Liquidity volume:** It is recommended to keep an amount equivalent to 2 to 3 months of living expenses minimum in cash.

- **Accessibility:** Make sure your cash is available and easily accessible whenever you need to use it, whether in a bank account or in cash at home.

9. Long-term financial planning

Long-term financial planning can protect you from future financial crises. By creating a financial plan that spans years, you can set financial goals such as buying a home, educating children, or retiring. Some important steps in financial planning include:

- **Set clear financial goals:** Set your big financial goals and make a thoughtful plan to achieve them over the long term.

- **Review the plan periodically:** Review your financial plan regularly to ensure you are on the right track and to make adjustments as necessary based on changes in your financial situation.

10. Get financial advice

Sometimes you may need help from financial management or investment experts to protect you from financial crises. Getting financial advice from a certified financial advisor can provide you with guidance on how to manage your money effectively and achieve financial stability.

- **When do you need a financial advisor?** If you're having trouble budgeting, want to invest effectively, or need guidance around debt, getting financial counseling may be the right option for you.

Conclusion

Protecting yourself from financial crises requires advance planning and adopting wise financial strategies. By building an emergency fund, diversifying income sources, avoiding excessive debt, and investing in long-term assets, you can enhance your ability to withstand financial crises and achieve long-term financial stability. Effective and ongoing financial planning can also help you achieve your financial goals and protect your financial future.

How to make your savings work for you?

Saving money is an important step towards achieving financial security and economic stability, but it should not be limited to just collecting and saving money. To make your savings work for you, you must be smart about how you invest and use them to increase your wealth in the long term. In this article, we will discuss effective and innovative strategies to make your savings generate financial returns and help you reach your financial goals.

1. Invest in high-interest savings accounts.

The first step to getting the most out of your savings is to invest them in savings accounts that offer high interest rates. Many people deposit their savings in traditional bank accounts that offer very low or no interest rates. However, there are high-yield savings accounts that offer you higher interest rates on the money you deposit. These accounts can be useful if you want to keep your savings liquid while earning extra income without taking on too much risk.

- **Where do you find it?** Check out digital banks or financial institutions that offer high-interest savings accounts. You may find interest rates of up to 2% or more, compared to traditional accounts that may offer less than 0.1%.

2. Invest in Mutual Funds

If you want to diversify your savings in an innovative way, you can invest in mutual funds. These funds pool the money of many investors and invest it in a variety of stocks and bonds, reducing the risk for individuals. The returns depend on the performance of the assets in which the fund invests.

- **Benefits of mutual funds:** These funds provide good diversification, as you can invest in hundreds of stocks or bonds through a single fund. They are also suitable for investors who do not have the time or knowledge to manage their own investments.

- **Types of funds:** There are mutual funds that are based on stocks, bonds, or both. There are also funds that invest in specific sectors such as technology, energy, or health.

3. Invest in real estate

Real estate is one of the most stable and profitable investments in the long term. You can use your savings to buy a property and rent it out or even sell it for a profit after a period of time. Real estate usually increases in value over time, making it a relatively safe investment.

Buying a property to rent: If you have enough money, you can buy an apartment or house and rent it out for a steady monthly income. This investment can be stable especially if you live in an area with a high demand for rentals.

Investing in real estate investment funds (REITs): If you don't want to actually buy a property, you can invest in real estate investment trusts. These funds invest in real estate assets and distribute profits to investors.

4. Start a small business

If you have a passion or a specific business idea, you can use your savings to start your own business. This could be an online store, a service-oriented business, or even the production and sale of handicrafts. Starting a small business is an effective way to turn your savings into a steady source of income over time.

- **Step one:** Before you start, make sure to conduct a feasibility study to determine if your idea is feasible and how much capital you need. You can start small and scale up as you make profits.

- **Risks and rewards:** Although small businesses can be risky, they offer the opportunity to innovate and make big profits if you are successful in managing your business.

5. Investing in education and self-development

One of the best ways to invest your savings is to spend it on developing your skills and knowledge. Self-education increases your chances of earning a higher income and increasing your potential in the job market. Whether you want to improve your current skills or learn something new, investing in yourself is always a wise decision.

- **Training courses and certificates:** You can invest part of your savings in obtaining training courses or professional certificates that increase your value in the job market. These courses can be in your current field or in new fields such as technology, programming, or digital marketing.

- **Online learning:** There are many platforms that offer high-quality courses at affordable prices. Some courses may be free or require a relatively small investment, but they open up great opportunities for you in the long run.

6. Investing in Dividend Stocks

Dividend paying stocks are one of the investments that allow you to earn a steady income from your savings. These stocks give you a percentage of the company's profits on a regular basis, providing you with a continuous income even if you do not sell the stocks.

- **How to choose:** Choose large, stable companies that operate in key industries and pay dividends to their shareholders on a regular basis. Companies with a good reputation and financial stability tend to pay large, sustainable dividends.

- **Additional benefit:** In addition to dividends, the value of the stock may rise over time, which means you may make an additional profit when you sell the stock in the future.

7. Investing in Cryptocurrency

Cryptocurrencies such as Bitcoin and Ethereum have become modern investment tools that many people resort to in order to achieve great returns on their savings. Although this type of investment may be risky due to market volatility, it can be an opportunity to achieve huge returns if handled carefully.

- **Start with caution:** If you are new to cryptocurrencies, it is best to start with small amounts of your savings and learn the market gradually. Investing in cryptocurrencies should be a small part of your investment portfolio, as the market can be very volatile.

- **Technology and the future:** Cryptocurrencies are based on blockchain technology, which is a technology that may have a major impact on many sectors in the future. Therefore, investing in cryptocurrencies may be a bet on the future, but you should always follow risk management strategies.

8. Investing in government or corporate bonds

Bonds are considered one of the safest and most stable financial instruments. When you invest in bonds, you lend money to the government or companies for a certain period of time and earn interest in return. Bonds provide a fixed income and are less risky than other investments.

- **Types of bonds:** You can invest in government bonds, which are considered the safest, or corporate bonds, which may offer higher returns but with greater risk.

- **Fixed income:** Bonds provide you with a steady cash flow in the form of interest, and are suitable for individuals who want to achieve financial stability without risking capital.

9. Use savings to purchase Certificates of Deposit (CDs)

Certificates of deposit are banking products that offer higher interest rates than regular savings accounts, but they require you to lock up your money for a certain period of time, ranging from a few months to several years. When the specified period ends, you get back the principal plus interest.

- **Benefits of certificates of deposit:** Certificates of deposit are an ideal option for those who want to secure their savings and get a fixed return without much risk.

- **Short or long term investment:** You can choose the period that suits your financial needs, whether you want to freeze your money for a short or long period.

10. Invest in yourself and your daily life.

Don't forget that investing part of your savings in improving your quality of life can have long-term financial benefits. Whether it's improving your health, strengthening your relationships, or even spending on things that bring you joy and peace of mind, these investments can make you more productive and more likely to achieve greater financial success.

- **For health and fitness:** Investing money in maintaining good health enhances your ability to work and be productive, thus increasing your chances of earning a higher income in the long run.

Conclusion

Turning your savings into a powerful tool for increasing your wealth requires innovative thinking and good planning. By investing in diverse assets such as real estate, stocks, and education, or even starting a small business, you can make your savings work for you and achieve financial security and sustainable growth. Using these methods strategically will ensure you achieve your financial goals and protect your financial future.

5. Section Five: Overcoming Debt

Effective Debt Repayment Strategies

Paying off debt effectively is a key goal for achieving financial freedom and economic stability. If you're drowning in debt, whether it's credit cards, personal loans, or any other type of financial obligation, creating an effective debt repayment plan can help you get out of it faster and less expensively. There are several strategies you can follow to pay off your debt effectively, and the best option for you depends on your financial situation and personal goals.

In this article, we will review 10 strategies for paying off debt effectively, with an explanation of how to apply each one to achieve the best results.

1. Identify and organize all debts.

The first step to paying off debt effectively is to accurately identify all of your debts and organize them in a way that allows you to see the big picture. The list should include:

- **Type of religion:** Whether it's credit card debt, a personal loan, a car loan, or a mortgage.

- **Amount due:** The total amount you must pay.

- **interest rate:** The higher the interest, the more money you pay in the long run.

- **Monthly installment:** The amount you pay each month for each debt.

This organization helps you set priorities and start making a plan to pay off debt in a regular and thoughtful way.

2. Use the Snowball Method

The snowball method is one of the most popular debt repayment strategies. This method involves paying off smaller debts first, then transferring the money that was earmarked for those debts to larger debts after they are paid off. The idea here is to create a psychological boost by paying off smaller debts quickly, which encourages you to continue.

- **How does it work?**
    a. Pay the minimum on each debt, except the smallest debt.
    b. Focus on paying off as much of the smaller debt as possible.
    c. After paying off the smallest debt, move on to the next one and so on.

- **Advantages:** This method helps build positive momentum by feeling a sense of accomplishment when you get rid of small debts quickly.

3. Use the Avalanche Method

Unlike the snowball method, the avalanche method involves paying off the highest-interest debts first. This method is more financially efficient because it helps you reduce the interest you pay in the long run.

- **How does it work?**

1. Pay the minimum on each debt.
2. Focus on paying off the debt with the highest interest rate with the largest amount possible.
3. Once you pay off the highest interest debt, move on to the next one and so on.

- **Advantages:** This method helps you reduce the total interest you pay, thus saving money in the long run.

4. Debt Consolidation

If you have multiple debts with high interest rates, you may want to consider debt consolidation. This option involves combining all of your debts into one loan with a lower interest rate. Instead of managing multiple monthly payments, you will have one payment with a lower interest rate.

- **How does it work?** You can apply for a debt consolidation loan from a bank or a financial company. This loan will help you pay off all your existing debts, and transfer all obligations into one payment.

- **Advantages:** Debt consolidation helps simplify the process and pay off debt with lower interest, allowing you to save money and get out of debt faster.

5. Negotiating with creditors

If you are having difficulty paying your debts, do not hesitate to contact your creditors and try to negotiate better terms. Some creditors may be willing to offer lower interest rates or extend the repayment period.

- **How does it work?** Contact your creditors and explain your financial situation. You may have the option to lower your monthly payments or even reduce the amount of debt owed.

- **Advantages:** Negotiating helps you reduce the financial burden and make monthly payments more affordable.

6. Use emergency savings carefully.

If you have good emergency savings, you can consider using them to pay off part of your debt. However, this should be a last resort option, as you should still have enough savings to deal with emergencies.

- **How does it work?** Use a portion of your emergency savings to pay off high-interest debt, but be sure not to cut your savings too much.

- **Advantages:** This option helps you get rid of some debt quickly and save money that you would have paid in interest.

7. Increase income to speed up repayment

Increasing your income can be an effective way to speed up the debt repayment process. You can look for additional jobs, freelance work, or use your skills to generate additional income. This additional income can be used entirely to pay off debt.

- **How does it work?** Allocate all of the extra income to paying off debt, allowing you to significantly reduce the repayment period.

- **Advantages:** This approach allows you to pay off debt faster while reducing the interest you pay in the long run.

8. Use bonuses and rewards to pay off debt.

If you get a bonus or raise from work, instead of spending it on luxuries, consider using it to pay off part of your debt. This can help you shorten your repayment period and reduce interest.

- **How does it work?** Instead of using rewards to spend, invest them in paying off as much debt as possible.

- **Advantages:** Reduce the amount owed and pay off debts faster.

9. Control unnecessary spending

Controlling unnecessary spending is a crucial part of your debt repayment plan. If you're overspending on unnecessary things, you may need to set a tight budget and focus on cutting back on that type of spending.

- **How does it work?** Review your monthly expenses and identify areas where you can cut back. Shift the money you used to spend on luxuries to debt repayment.

- **Advantages:** Reducing expenses allows you to direct more money toward debt repayment, which shortens the repayment period.

10. Consult a financial expert

If you are struggling to manage your debt on your own, it can be helpful to seek the help of a financial advisor. A financial advisor can help you develop a clear plan for paying off your debt and offer advice on how to better manage your money.

- **How does it work?** Find a licensed financial advisor and sit down to discuss your financial situation. He or she will analyze your debts and financial resources, and guide you on appropriate debt repayment strategies.
- **Advantages:** Financial counseling helps you organize your debts and achieve your financial goals in more effective ways.

Conclusion

Effective debt repayment requires good planning and long-term commitment. By following these strategies, you can reduce the interest you pay and speed up the process of paying off your debt. The most important thing is to stick with the plan you choose and not give up. By following these tips, you will be able to achieve greater financial freedom and regain control of your financial life.

Negotiating with creditors and alleviating financial burdens

Negotiating with creditors is a crucial step in easing financial burdens and achieving financial stability. Whether you are struggling to pay your debts or want to relieve the pressure of high interest, negotiating with creditors can help you create flexible debt repayment plans and improve your financial situation. In this article, we will discuss in detail how to negotiate with creditors, the benefits of this step, and the most important tips to follow to get the most out of this process.

The importance of negotiating with creditors

Negotiating with creditors can help you avoid bankruptcy or further financial accumulation that may make repayment more difficult. By communicating directly with creditors, agreements can be reached that ensure you are able to pay your debts comfortably without significantly impacting your daily life or overall financial situation. Some creditors may be willing to offer creative solutions such as debt installment or lower interest rates based on your financial situation.

When should you negotiate with creditors?

There are several circumstances that may prompt you to consider negotiating with creditors:

1-When you are unable to pay the minimum monthly payments: If you find yourself unable to make the minimum monthly payments on your debts, it is best to contact your creditors as soon as possible to avoid further fines or penalties.

2-When interest rates rise significantly: Sometimes, high interest rates can significantly increase your debt burden. Negotiating a lower interest rate or extending your repayment period may help you ease this burden.

3-When you face temporary financial pressures: Job loss, or unexpected costs such as medical expenses, can impact your ability to repay debt. Negotiating with creditors to provide temporary solutions, such as deferring or reducing payments for a set period, can be helpful.

Effective strategies for negotiating with creditors

Before you start negotiating with creditors, there are some important steps to take to ensure the success of the process:

1. **Analyze your financial situation clearly** Before negotiating, carefully review your financial situation. Determine your total monthly income, expenses, and debts. You should have a clear idea of how much you can set aside each month to pay off your debts. This analysis will help you make a realistic and reasonable offer to your creditors.

2. **Contact your creditors as soon as possible.** When you feel like you won't be able to make payments on time, don't wait until the problem becomes serious.

Contact your creditors as soon as possible and ask them to discuss flexible payment options. Creditors often prefer to work with debtors who are willing to communicate and resolve the issue.

3. **Be honest and specific.** When communicating with creditors, be honest about your financial situation and provide specific details about the difficulties you are facing. Transparency here is important to build trust between you and your creditors. They may understand your situation and offer appropriate solutions if they feel that you are committed and really want to repay the debt.

4. **Be prepared to make a realistic presentation.** After you have reviewed your financial situation, make a reasonable offer to creditors based on your actual ability to repay. The offer may be to lower your interest rate, spread payments over a longer period of time, or defer payments for a specified period until your financial circumstances improve.

5. **Negotiating interest rates** One of the most important aspects of negotiating is trying to lower your interest rate. If you have high-interest debt, this extra burden

may make it difficult for you to pay it off. Negotiating a lower interest rate can significantly reduce the total amount you have to pay off, making your monthly payments more manageable.

6. **Consider debt consolidation**Debt consolidation is an option where you can combine all of your debts into one monthly payment with lower interest. If you feel like you have multiple debts that are making it difficult to manage, debt consolidation may be an option worth negotiating with your creditors.

7. **Debt rescheduling request**If you're having trouble paying your debts, you can request a debt rescheduling. This means extending your repayment period, which reduces the amount you pay each month. Of course, this may mean you'll be paying interest for a longer period, but it can be a good temporary option to relieve financial stress.

8. **Consider paying off part of the debt directly.**Sometimes, creditors may be willing to accept a partial payment instead of the full amount if you are unable to pay the full amount. This option is known as a "partial settlement," and occurs when

both parties agree on a specific amount to settle the entire debt. This option can be attractive if you have a sum of money but cannot afford to pay the entire debt.

Benefits of Negotiating with Creditors

Negotiating with creditors can have significant benefits, including:

1- Reducing the financial burden: Negotiating a lower interest rate or debt restructuring can reduce the daily financial stress you face, and give you more breathing room in managing your money.

2- Maintain your credit rating: Instead of defaulting or being late with payments, negotiating with creditors can preserve your credit rating, as defaulting on payments can result in a negative record on your credit report.

3- Avoid bankruptcy: In some cases, negotiating with creditors may help you avoid more drastic action such as bankruptcy, which could have long-lasting effects on your financial situation.

4- Increased flexibility in payment: By negotiating, you can get lower monthly payments or a longer repayment period, making the debt more manageable.

Tips for Successful Negotiation with Creditors

1- Do not ignore the problem: If you know that repaying a debt will be difficult, don't avoid creditors or delay communicating with them. Be proactive.

2- Use a respectful tone: When communicating with creditors, be sure to use a respectful and frank tone. Being resentful or aggressive will not help achieve resolution.

3-Be realistic: Don't make promises you can't keep. It's better to be realistic about what you can offer than to try to temporarily satisfy creditors.

4- Be prepared to negotiate: Don't expect creditors to accept all of your terms right away. Negotiation is a process that requires compromise from both sides, so be prepared to listen and discuss.

5- Consult a financial advisor: If you feel the situation is complicated or you are unsure how to negotiate, it may be helpful to speak to a professional financial advisor who can help you through the process.

Conclusion

Negotiating with creditors is a powerful tool to ease financial burdens and improve your financial situation. By following the right strategies, you can get flexible solutions that will help you pay off your debts in a comfortable manner. The most important thing is to start at the right time and communicate honestly with creditors to ensure you reach the best possible solutions.

How to Avoid Falling into Debt Again

Falling into a debt trap is an experience that can be very damaging to one's financial and psychological well-being. Getting out of debt is a significant accomplishment, but it is not complete without ensuring that you do not fall into it again. If you have already gotten out of debt or are trying to get out of it, being careful and having clear strategies in place is the key to ensuring that you do not fall back into this trap again.

In this article, we will discuss 10 effective ways you can follow to avoid falling into the debt trap again and achieve lasting financial stability.

1. Assess the current financial situation

The first step to avoiding falling back into debt is to objectively assess your current financial situation. Reflect on how far you've come, and identify weak points in your budget that could lead to more debt in the future.

- **Revenue and Expense Analysis**Create a comprehensive list of all your monthly income and expenses. Knowing your cash flow is key to understanding whether you are living within or beyond your means.

- **Reduce unnecessary expenses** Once you have identified all of your expenses, look at areas where you can cut costs. Some of these expenses may be unnecessary and can be eliminated or reduced.

2. Develop an accurate financial budget.

Creating a solid monthly budget is one of the most important ways you can avoid debt. A budget acts as a roadmap that helps you organize your income and spending effectively.

- **Priority analysis**: Set your financial priorities. You should start by covering basic expenses like rent, food, and transportation before thinking about spending on luxuries.

- **Strict adherence to budget**: After setting a budget, try to stick to it strictly. You may sometimes find yourself tempted to overspend, but maintaining your discipline is the key to avoiding debt.

3. Build a financial emergency fund

An emergency fund is your financial cushion in case of an unexpected event, such as a car repair, unexpected medical expenses, or job loss. Having this fund reduces your need to borrow money in difficult times.

- **Start saving gradually**: You don't need a large sum of money to start an emergency fund. You can start by saving a small portion of your income each month and gradually increase it over time.

- **Savings goal**Try to save enough to cover your basic expenses for three to six months. This amount provides you with a strong financial cushion against any emergency.

4. Avoid relying on credit cards.

Credit cards can be a double-edged sword. While they provide convenience when making payments, their irresponsible use can lead to debt.

- **Use cards with caution.**: Try to use your credit card only when you are able to pay the balance in full at the end of the month. Avoid deferring payments or paying only the minimum, as accruing interest can lead to significant debt.
- **Cancel unnecessary cards**If you have more than one credit card, you may want to cancel the ones you don't need to avoid temptations to overspend.

5. Set long-term financial goals

Setting clear financial goals helps you stay focused and avoid debt. Having a financial goal is a powerful motivator to stick to your budget and avoid overspending.

- **Setting savings goals** If you want to buy a house or a car, or invest in your children's education, make sure you have a financial plan that will ensure you achieve these goals without having to borrow.

- **Investing in the future**: Instead of relying on loans, invest your savings in achieving your financial goals. You can invest the money in high-interest savings accounts or long-term investments.

6. Avoid buying on credit.

One of the most common reasons for falling into a debt trap is buying on credit or installments. Buying things on credit may seem like an easy solution at first, but it can lead to accumulating financial obligations.

- **Cash payment when possible**: Try to pay for purchases in cash whenever possible. This will make you realize how much each purchase affects your budget and prevent you from overspending.

- **Think before you buy** Before deciding to buy something on credit, think carefully about whether you really need it, and whether you can afford to pay cash in the future.

7. Monitor expenses constantly.

Controlling your spending is key to staying out of debt. You need to track how you spend your money regularly and identify areas where you can cut back.

- **Record daily expenses** You can use apps or a notebook to record your daily expenses. This will help you see where your money is going, and if there are areas you can improve.

- **Review budget monthly**: Make sure to review your budget each month and update it as needed. This review will give you the opportunity to make sure you are on the right track and avoiding debt.

8. Improving financial awareness and financial education

Investing in learning more about finances helps you avoid falling into the debt trap. Understanding the basics of financial management and investing helps you make informed financial decisions.

- **Read financial books and articles** There are many books and articles that offer advice on personal financial management. Learning from the experiences of others can provide you with valuable tips for avoiding debt.

- **Attend financial courses** If you need more financial knowledge, you can sign up for online courses or attend workshops that will help you better manage your money.

9. Diversify sources of income

Relying on one source of income can be risky, especially if you face financial crises or lose your job. Therefore, it is necessary to look for ways to increase and diversify your income.

- **Find side jobs** If you have the time, you can work a side job or do freelance work to supplement your income.

- **Investing in existing skills** You can also improve your skills to get better job opportunities or increase your income through promotions at work.

10. Manage existing debt effectively

If you still carry some debt, you need to manage this debt wisely to avoid getting into even greater debt.

- **Pay off high interest debt first.** If you have high-interest debt, try to focus on paying it off first to reduce the interest cost.

- **Negotiating with creditors** If you are having difficulty paying your debts, do not hesitate to negotiate with your creditors to request a reduction in interest or arrange an easy repayment plan.

a summary

Staying out of the debt trap requires a well-thought-out financial plan, building healthy financial habits, and sticking to a strict budget. By avoiding debt, controlling spending, and planning for the future, you can ensure lasting financial stability and achieve your financial goals without having to fall back into the debt trap.

story

In the yearIn 2010, Sarah was living in a small town with a steady job, but she found herself drowning in debt. Things started to get worse when she bought a new car with a huge loan, and she piled on more and more credit cards to finance unnecessary expenses, like vacations and luxury purchases. Over time, the debt piled up to the point where she couldn't manage it. Each month, most of her paycheck went to interest payments, while the principal balances on the loans were barely touched.

The Beginning: Sliding into Debt

Sarah initially didn't realize how dangerous debt was. She saw credit cards as a convenient way to buy what she needed without thinking about the consequences. She started buying new furniture for her house and took a luxurious vacation that she thought she deserved after years of hard work. Over time, she started using more cards to buy unnecessary things, not realizing that debt was accumulating at high interest rates.

Things came to a head when she suddenly lost her job due to staff cuts at her company. She was living without a steady source of income, and at the same time, she was receiving daily calls from banks and credit card companies demanding debt repayment. Sarah felt helpless and frustrated, not knowing how she could ever get over the huge mountain of debt she had incurred.

Facing reality

At one point in time, Sarah sat down to review her financial life. She was depressed and living in constant fear of losing her home and car. But in that moment, she realized that denying or ignoring the problem would not help her overcome her debt. She decided that she needed to radically change the way she managed her money and face her financial reality with courage.

Sarah began to assess the actual amount of debt she had. She sat down and wrote down everything she owed on credit cards, personal loans, a car loan, and any other debt. She was shocked to see that the total amount of debt was more than $50,000, an amount you never expected.

Make a debt repayment plan

After realizing the magnitude of the problem, Sarah decided it was time to put together a strict debt repayment plan. She began reading books and articles about personal finance and how to get out of debt, and through her research, she learned about two basic ways to get out of debt: **snowball method** and **Avalanche method**.

Snowball method:

This method is based on starting by paying off the smallest debt first, in order to motivate the person to continue with the process. After paying off the smallest debt, you move on to the next debt and so on, while continuing to make the minimum payments on the rest of the debts. The goal of this method is to achieve small successes that motivate the person to continue with his plan.

Avalanche method:

On the other hand, the avalanche method requires a person to pay off the highest-interest debt first. This method is more financially efficient because it helps reduce the total cost of interest a person pays over time. However, it can be less motivating than the snowball method, because high-interest debt is often larger in amount and takes longer to pay off.

Sarah decided to follow **Avalanche method** Because she wanted to get rid of the high interest that was weighing her down. She started paying off the credit cards that had the highest interest rates, while continuing to make minimum payments on the rest of the debt. Her main goal was to reduce the total interest she was paying and increase what she could save in the long run.

Reduce expenses and increase income

In addition to the debt repayment plan, Sarah realized that she needed to make a radical change in her financial lifestyle. She decided that she needed to live frugally so that she could pay off her debts faster. She took a number of radical steps to reduce her expenses:

1. **give up luxuries** Sarah decided that she would give up luxury vacations and unnecessary purchases. She stopped using credit cards for her daily needs and decided that she would not buy anything new unless it was absolutely necessary.

2. **Selling non-essential assets** She sold her new car and bought a smaller, cheaper car that used less fuel. She also sold many of the luxury furniture she had previously purchased and considered unnecessary.

3. **Find additional sources of income** Sarah sought to supplement her income in various ways. She started freelancing online offering writing and editing services. She also did private tutoring in her spare time to supplement her income.

Challenges on the road

Overcoming debt wasn't easy. There were moments of frustration and despair when she felt the process was too slow. Sometimes she wondered if she would ever be able to overcome this financial burden. But she was determined to succeed.

When she was facing challenges, she would turn to reading success stories of others who had overcome their debt, which gave her the mental boost to keep going. She also set herself small rewards when she was making progress in paying off debt, such as celebrating with a simple dinner when she finished paying off a certain debt.

Success in the end

After four years of sticking to her strict plan, Sarah was able to pay off all of her debt. She felt incredibly happy when she made the final payment on her last credit card. She was rid of the mountain of debt that had been weighing her down for years, and her financial life was back on track.

Lessons learned

1. **Recognizing the problem is the first step.** Sarah was only able to overcome her debt after she faced reality and realized the magnitude of the problem. Denying or ignoring the problem only makes the situation worse.

2. **Having a plan is key.** Without a structured plan, Sarah would have continued to live in debt.

Thoughtful financial plans like the Avalanche Method helped her regain control of her finances.

3. **Short-term sacrifice for long-term success**: Sacrificing luxuries and living frugally for a period of time allowed Sarah to free herself from debt faster. The temporary sacrifice led to lasting financial freedom.

4. **Patience and commitment**Getting out of debt is not something that can be achieved overnight. Patience and sticking to the plan were the keys to Sarah's success.

5. **Increased income boosts plan**Finding additional sources of income was an important part of Sarah's success. She not only relied on reducing expenses, but also sought to increase income to pay off debts faster.

Conclusion

Sarah's story highlights how someone who was drowning in debt could overcome her financial situation by sticking to a solid plan and living frugally for a period of time. By confronting the problem and developing a clear plan to reduce expenses and increase income, she was able to achieve financial freedom and get rid of the debt that was weighing her down.

6. Section Six: Financial Freedom

What is financial freedom and how to achieve it?

Financial freedom is a financial state that an individual achieves when they have enough assets and savings to cover their personal expenses without having to rely on a steady job income. In this case, the person can make their financial decisions freely and without worrying about not having enough money to meet their needs. Simply put, financial freedom means having the ability to enjoy life without being tied down by the pressure of debt or constantly worrying about daily expenses.

In this article, we will discuss the concept of financial freedom and the importance of achieving it, then review the basic steps to reach this financial state that many aspire to.

The importance of financial freedom

Financial freedom gives individuals the ability to have complete control over their lives and time. A person who achieves financial freedom does not have to work long hours or in jobs that do not meet their ambitions just to survive financially. The most prominent benefits of financial freedom are:

- **get rid of financial anxiety**Many people are constantly worried about not being able to pay their bills or facing financial emergencies. Financial freedom provides security and peace of mind about your financial future.

- **Full control of time**When you achieve financial freedom, you have the ability to choose how to spend your time, whether working on projects you love or enjoying your personal and family life.

- **Achieving personal goals** With financial freedom, you can focus on achieving your life goals and ambitions without the financial pressure that may hinder these goals.

Steps to achieve financial freedom

Achieving financial freedom is not easy, but it is possible with a solid financial plan, commitment, and long-term patience. Here are the basic steps you can take to achieve financial freedom:

1. Control expenses and build an effective budget

The first step towards financial freedom is to have complete control over your expenses and create an effective monthly budget. You need to know how to allocate your income in a smart way that prevents you from overspending.

- **Recording expenses**: Track all your monthly expenses, including small ones that may seem insignificant. This detail helps you see where your money is going and identify areas where you can cut back.

- **reduce unnecessary expenses** After recording expenses, identify luxuries and unnecessary spending. Try to reduce these expenses and focus on meeting basic needs and saving.

2. Get rid of debt

One of the biggest barriers to financial freedom is debt. When you are burdened with debt, a large portion of your income goes toward paying off these obligations, reducing your ability to save and invest.

- **Pay off high interest debt first.** If you have multiple debts, start by paying off the highest-interest debts first. This will help you reduce the interest you accrue in the long run.

- **Negotiating with creditors** If you are having difficulty paying off your debts, try negotiating with your creditors to lower interest or arrange a more favorable repayment plan.

3. Build a financial emergency fund

Having an emergency fund is essential to achieving financial freedom, as it helps you deal with unexpected expenses such as car repairs or medical bills without having to go into debt.

- Gradual savings: Try to set aside a portion of your monthly income to build an emergency fund. The goal is to have enough to cover your basic expenses for at least three to six months.

4. Smart investment

Investing is one of the keys to achieving financial freedom. Instead of relying solely on your job income, you can invest your money to grow it and increase its returns over time.

- Long-term investing: Focus on investing in assets that grow over time such as stocks, real estate, or bonds. Avoid high-risk investments that could result in significant financial losses.

- Diversify your investment portfolio: It is important to diversify your investments to reduce risk. Instead of putting all your money in one type of asset, try spreading it across several different investment categories.

5. Diversify sources of income

Relying on a single source of income may not be enough to achieve financial freedom. Therefore, it is beneficial to look for ways to diversify your income sources to increase returns and achieve greater financial stability.

- Side jobs or small business investment: You can look for side job opportunities to supplement your income. Additionally, starting a small business can be an additional source of income.

6. Regular savings

One of the most important habits that will bring you closer to financial freedom is the habit of regular saving.

The more you save, the more chances you have to achieve financial freedom.

- Allocate a percentage of your income to savings: Try to allocate a percentage of your monthly income to savings. This percentage may be 10% or 20% depending on your financial circumstances. The important thing is to continue saving regularly.

7. Learn financial planning and investing

Financial awareness is one of the most important factors in achieving financial freedom. The more you learn about financial planning and investing, the more you will be able to make smart financial decisions.

- Reading and learning: Invest your time in reading financial books and articles, and attending training courses that help you improve your financial skills.

8. Patience and financial discipline

Achieving financial freedom takes time, patience, and constant commitment. It may take years, but financial discipline and consistency in the plan will eventually lead to achieving your desired goals.

- Stay away from temptations: Avoid financial temptations that may lead to overspending or debt. You must remain committed to your financial goals and always be aware of the consequences of ill-considered financial decisions.

Conclusion

Financial freedom is the ability to control your financial life without relying on a steady source of income or loans. To achieve it, it requires setting a budget, getting rid of debt, investing wisely, and saving money regularly. With patience and discipline, you can achieve financial freedom and enjoy a life free of financial stress.

The importance of multiple sources of income

In today's world, the importance of diversifying income streams is becoming increasingly apparent. Relying on a single source of income may seem sufficient to some at first, but many people are hit with sudden financial shocks when their primary source of income changes unexpectedly. This shift in thinking towards income diversification is not only about providing financial protection, but it is also in line with the concept of financial independence and achieving financial freedom.

In this article, we will discuss the importance of diversifying income streams, the benefits this strategy can offer, and how to effectively start building additional income streams.

1. Protection from financial risks

Relying on a single income can be very risky. You may lose your job or your income may decrease for any reason, whether it is due to external economic factors such as financial crises or even personal changes such as illness or retirement. This is where having multiple sources of income comes in as it provides you with a financial safety net that protects you from being completely dependent on one source only.

- **Reduce risk** Having more than one source of income makes your financial situation less vulnerable to sudden financial shocks. If you lose one source of income, you will still have other sources to cover your expenses and maintain financial stability.

- **avoid getting into debt** In the event of the loss of a primary source of income, people who rely on one source may find themselves having to borrow money to cover their basic expenses. In contrast, those who rely on multiple sources of income can avoid resorting to debt.

2. Increase income and achieve financial goals

When diversifying income sources, the goal is not only to reduce risk, but also to increase the overall income level. People who have multiple income sources can earn much higher incomes compared to those who rely solely on their monthly salaries.

- **Investing in personal goals** By increasing your income, you can accelerate the achievement of your financial goals, such as buying a home, investing in your children's education, or even saving for retirement. The additional income can also be used to boost your investments and grow your wealth over the long term.

- **improve standard of living** Increasing your sources of income allows you to improve your standard of living without having to sacrifice much. You may be able to afford travel, entertainment, or developing new skills that you have been avoiding due to tight budgets.

3. Financial independence and financial freedom

Diversifying your income streams can be a major step toward achieving financial independence. Relying on one income makes your life too tied to a specific job or company, leaving you constantly under work pressure and worried about losing your job.

- **Financial independence** By having multiple sources of income, you can reduce your dependence on one job or one boss. You can make more independent career decisions, and you may be able to work in a field you love or start your own business without worrying about financial losses.

- **Financial freedom** The ultimate goal of diversifying your income streams is to achieve financial freedom. Financial freedom means being able to cover all your expenses without having to work full-time, with the returns from your investments and side projects being enough to secure a sustainable lifestyle.

4. Develop skills and increase personal value

When you start looking for additional sources of income, you will find yourself having to learn new skills or improve your current ones. You may learn how to run a small business, invest your money in real estate or stocks, or even improve your skills in other areas.

- **Increase personal value** By diversifying your income streams, you become more adaptable to changes in the job market. Developing new skills or gaining different experiences makes you more valuable in the job market, increasing your chances of getting better jobs or achieving more success in your own projects.

- **Developing entrepreneurship skills** Many people who start diversifying their income streams eventually find themselves running small businesses or freelancing. This experience enhances entrepreneurial and leadership skills, opening up greater opportunities for the future.

5. Increase financial security in retirement

When they retire, many people rely on a pension or savings they have built up over their working years. But pensions are often not enough to cover growing living expenses or deal with economic changes.

- **Earn extra income in retirement** If you start building multiple income streams before retirement, it gives you the ability to generate additional income even in your retirement years. Investments in real estate, stocks, or even side hustles can be a significant source of ongoing income.

- **Maintaining the standard of living** By diversifying your income streams, you can ensure that you will be able to maintain or improve your current standard of living during your retirement years.

6. Build wealth faster

When you rely on a single source of income, your ability to build wealth may be limited. However, diversifying your income gives you the opportunity to grow your assets and wealth faster.

- **Investing additional revenue** Additional income can be invested in financial assets such as stocks, real estate, or even starting a small business. This helps build wealth in the long term and increases the chances of achieving financial independence.

- **Diversification of investments**: Income diversification gives you the opportunity to diversify your investments. For example, you can invest part of your income in real estate and another in the stock market. This diversification reduces risk and increases the chances of achieving high returns.

7. Preparing for emergencies and crises

Life is full of surprises, and no one can predict economic crises or sudden changes that may affect their income. Having multiple sources of income enhances your ability to deal with financial crises and emergencies more effectively.

- **Covering emergency expenses** When you have more than one source of income, you are in a better position to cover emergency expenses like home repairs or medical bills without having to go into debt.

- **Stability in economic crises** In the event of an economic crisis that affects one of your sources of income, having other sources can ensure the continued flow of money and reduce the impact of the crisis on your daily life.

How do you start building multiple streams of income?

1- Start looking for freelance opportunities If you have skills that can be offered freely such as design, writing, programming, or even teaching, you can start offering your services on the side.

2-Invest in assets: Start thinking about investing in assets such as stocks, bonds, or real estate. These investments can generate steady income over time.

3-Create a side project If you are passionate about a small business idea, you can start a side project without having to leave your current job. This could be an online business idea or a small store.

4-Invest in learning and development: Gaining new skills can open doors to new sources of income. Learn a new field or earn professional certifications that will boost your value in the job market.

Conclusion

Diversifying your income streams is not just a way to avoid financial risk, it's a strategy for building financial independence and increasing wealth. By creating multiple streams of income, you can enhance your financial security, achieve your personal goals, and prepare for any crises you may face in the future. It starts with simple steps like looking for additional income opportunities and investing time in learning the necessary skills, allowing you to take control of your financial future and achieve financial freedom.

How to build investments that make you financially free?

Financial freedom is a dream that many people strive for, and smart investments are one of the most important ways to achieve this goal. Achieving financial freedom means being able to cover your basic expenses and achieve a comfortable standard of living without having to work all the time. Investing is the primary way to build wealth and achieve financial independence, but achieving this goal requires knowledge, careful planning, and long-term patience.

In this article, we'll explore how to build strong, sustainable investments that will enable you to achieve financial freedom, focusing on key strategies and practical steps you can take.

1. Understanding the concept of investment

Before you start building investments that will make you financially free, it is important to understand what investing means. Investing is simply the allocation of capital into assets or projects with the goal of generating long-term financial returns. Investment assets include real estate, stocks, bonds, gold, and other instruments that can increase the value of capital over time.

- **Capital development** The main goal of investing is to achieve capital growth over time. By investing in assets that increase in value over time, you can increase your wealth without having to work for money.

- **Diversity and Sustainability** One of the most important principles of successful investment is diversifying the investment portfolio to ensure sustainability. Diversification reduces risks and increases the chances of achieving profitable returns.

2. Setting financial goals

Before you start building investments, you need to clearly define your financial goals. These goals should be realistic and measurable, as they will help you make the right decisions about the type of investments that are right for you. For example, do you want to achieve financial freedom in ten years? Or would you prefer to build a large retirement fund?

- **Time frame** You need to determine the time frame in which you want to achieve your goals. Some investments take a long time to achieve their returns, such as real estate or stocks, while other investments may achieve faster returns, such as business ventures.

- **Risk level** Every type of investment carries a certain level of risk. You need to be honest with yourself about your financial risk tolerance. Some people prefer high risks in exchange for high returns, while others prefer safe, steady investments.

3. Start saving for investment

To start your investment journey, you must have enough capital to start investing. This is where saving comes in. You should allocate a portion of your monthly income to saving on a regular basis until you have an amount that can be invested.

- **Create a monthly budget**: Set a clear budget that allows you to save regularly. Try to reduce unnecessary expenses and increase savings directed towards investment.

- **Create an emergency fund** Before you start investing, make sure you build a financial emergency fund that will cover your expenses for a period of 3-6 months minimum. This fund will provide you with protection in case of any financial emergency and prevent you from withdrawing from your investments.

4. Diversification of investments

One of the most important principles of building strong investments is diversifying your investment portfolio. Diversification means spreading your investments across several different asset classes to reduce risk and increase your chances of achieving good returns. If you invest all your money in one type of asset, you expose yourself to great risks if the value of that asset declines.

- **Stocks** Investing in stocks can be a powerful way to build wealth over the long term. Stocks represent a stake in a company, allowing you to profit from the growth of that company over time. However, you should be aware that the market can be volatile, which means there may be fluctuations in the value of your investments.

- **Real Estate**: Investing in real estate is a safe and sustainable way to generate steady rental income or increase the value of your property over the long term. Real estate is a tangible asset and has a lower risk profile than stocks.

- **Bonds**Bonds are relatively safe investment instruments, as they allow you to earn a steady income from interest. Bonds are suitable for those who want to preserve their capital while generating sustainable income.

- **Gold and other assets**Gold is a defensive asset, retaining its value even during economic downturns. The portfolio can also be diversified by investing in other instruments such as cryptocurrencies or raw materials depending on market trends.

5. Investing in yourself

One of the most important ways to build strong investments is to invest in yourself. Continuous learning and developing personal and professional skills can increase your ability to make wise investment decisions and enhance your long-term potential.

- **Financial Education**: You should always strive to learn more about financial planning and investing. Understanding the market and the basics of investing will help you make informed decisions. You can read books, attend seminars, or enroll in online courses to enhance your knowledge.

- **Develop professional skills**Investing in developing your professional skills can increase your base income, allowing you to allocate more money to invest. The more qualified you are in your field, the more opportunities you have to increase your income and achieve financial freedom.

6. Risk control

Investing always involves risks, but what distinguishes a successful investor is the ability to control and manage these risks effectively. You must be prepared to face the fluctuations and challenges that you may encounter in your investment journey.

- **Portfolio diversification** As mentioned earlier, diversification is the most effective way to reduce risk. Don't put all your eggs in one basket, but spread your investments across several asset classes.

- **Portfolio re-evaluation** You should review your investment portfolio periodically to ensure that it remains consistent with your financial goals and risk tolerance. You may need to adjust the portfolio based on changes in the market or your personal goals.

- **Long term investment**: Avoid getting involved in short-term investments or quick profit attempts. The best investments are those that are built for the long term and allow you to benefit from the growth of assets over time.

7. Investing residual income

Instead of spending any extra income that comes in, you should allocate a large portion of it to reinvestment. This step is what distinguishes successful investors, as they use the proceeds to generate further growth.

- **reinvestment of profits** If you are making profits from your current investments, whether from stock returns or property rentals, you should reinvest a portion of those profits to grow your portfolio further.

- **Focus on compound returns** One of the most powerful wealth-building strategies is to take advantage of compounding returns. The more you reinvest dividends, the faster your investments grow over time, allowing you to earn greater returns.

8. Patience and persistence

Building investments that will make you financially free doesn't happen overnight. It takes years of work, commitment, and patience. Investing success requires sticking to your financial and investment plan even during times when things may seem difficult or discouraging.

- **Avoid giving in to market fluctuations.** The financial market can be volatile at times, but you must stay consistent and stick to your investment strategy. Remember, long-term investing is what will bring real results.

- **be patient** You must accept that building wealth and financial freedom takes time. Results will not come quickly, but if you stick to your plan and follow wise investment strategies, you will achieve your financial goals in the long run.

Conclusion

Building strong, sustainable investments is the key to achieving financial freedom. By setting your financial goals, starting to save, diversifying your investment portfolio, and controlling risk, you can build wealth that will allow you to become financially independent. With commitment and patience, you will be able to achieve the financial freedom you dream of and enjoy a life free of financial worries.

story

In the year 2005, Omar was an ambitious young man working in a medium-sized company after graduating from university. He was earning a steady income that met his daily needs, but his ambition was beyond just a monthly salary. He had always heard about the concept of **Financial freedom**, a state in which a person is able to cover the costs of living without having to work for money. But at the time, he didn't know exactly how to get there. All he knew was that he didn't want to spend his life working just to pay the bills.

Getting Started: Discovery and Motivation

One day, Omar was reading a famous book called **Rich Dad Poor Dad** By Robert Kiyosaki. In this book, Omar finds a new philosophy about money and investing that is completely different from what he learned in college. The book talks about the importance of creating multiple streams of income and investing in assets that generate income instead of working just to increase income.

These thoughts sparked Omar. He felt excited and started thinking about how to transform his life from someone who relied on a steady job to someone who enjoyed financial freedom. He knew it wouldn't happen overnight, but he had the desire and dedication to make it happen.

Learning and planning

Omar took his first step towards financial freedom by:**Self-education**He started reading every book he could get his hands on about investing, money management, and wealth creation. He attended workshops, took online courses, and networked with successful people in the fields of investing and entrepreneurship. He realized that a proper understanding of money was the foundation of any journey toward financial independence.

After years of learning, Omar came up with a solid plan. The first thing he realized was that working alone is not enough to achieve financial freedom.**Investing in assets**That generates long-term income. Assets include real estate, stocks, bonds, and any other investment that can generate passive income, meaning the money works for him without the need for direct daily intervention.

First Steps: Investing in Real Estate

Omar decided to start first in **Real estate investment**, as he believed that this field had the potential to generate a steady and continuous income. He collected part of his personal savings and borrowed an additional amount from the bank to buy his first property, a small apartment in a middle-class neighborhood. The apartment needed some repairs, so he made the necessary modifications and then rented it out.

The income he got from renting out the apartment was the first step towards financial freedom. This money came in every month without him having to work for it directly. He began to feel that this was the right path.

Omar did not settle for one apartment, but continued to buy properties gradually. Whenever he saved an additional amount from his savings or from the income he received from rent, he invested it in buying a new property. After several years, he owned several properties that provided him with a steady income.

Diversify sources of income

Despite his success in real estate, Omar understood the importance of **Diversify sources of income** He didn't want to rely solely on real estate, especially since markets could be volatile. So he started exploring other areas.

1. **Investing in stocks** Omar started buying stocks after learning more about the financial markets and how to pick high-value stocks. He wasn't buying stocks with the intention of selling them quickly for a quick profit, but rather investing in companies with promising futures to generate long-term returns. This approach was similar to his approach to real estate, where he wanted to make money work for him.

2. **create a side business** In addition to his investments, Omar also decided to start a side project. He started a small business that provided financial advice to young people who wanted to learn how to manage their money. The project didn't take a lot of time, but it was another way to diversify his income and increase his sources of income.

3. **Passive income from books and educational courses** After several years of success, Omar wrote a book about his journey to financial freedom and created an online course. This was a new source of passive income, as the book and course were

constantly selling without his need for a permanent presence.

Expense control and smart planning

A key part of Omar's success in achieving financial freedom was **Control expenses**He did not spend his money lavishly, but lived a modest life despite his greatly increased income. He believed that controlling expenses was as important as increasing income. Therefore, he made sure to prepare a precise personal budget that included everything he needed, and invested any surplus in income-generating assets.

In addition, he was constantly planning for the future. He did not rely on luck or random opportunities. Every investment decision was carefully considered based on long-term goals. This strategic planning helped him avoid taking big risks that could result in losing everything he had achieved.

Achieving financial freedom

After years of commitment to smart investing and developing his sources of income, Omar finally reached what he dreamed of: **Financial freedom** His income from investments and side hustles covered all of his expenses, and even left him with a large surplus that he could use to continue investing or to fund his personal travels and dreams. He no longer had to work for money, but money worked for him.

At the age of 40, Omar decided to retire from his regular job. He could now spend his time traveling the world, spending more time with his family and friends, or working on his own projects that he loved. He no longer had to worry about bills or daily expenses, as his investments were generating a steady and sustainable income.

Lessons learned

Omar's story holds many important lessons that anyone seeking to achieve financial freedom can benefit from:

1. **Education is the foundation** Omar initially had no financial experience, but he realized the importance of learning. Investing in knowledge can be the first step towards financial success.

2. **Long term planning** Financial freedom doesn't happen overnight. It took Omar years of planning and commitment to achieve his goal. Success requires vision and patience.

3. **Diversify sources of income**: Instead of relying on one source, Omar diversified his investments into real estate, stocks, and side projects. This helped him reduce risk and increase his chances of success.

4. **Control expenses** Financial success does not only depend on increasing income, but also requires careful control over expenses. Omar did not spend his money lavishly but was keen to invest any surplus.

5. **Investing in assets** Instead of focusing on luxuries, Omar invested in assets that would generate income for him in the long term.

Conclusion

Omar's story is a living example of how to achieve **Financial freedom** Through education, planning, and commitment. The road may seem long and difficult, but success is possible for those who have the vision and discipline to achieve their goals. Financial freedom is not just a distant dream, but a reality that can be reached through thoughtful steps and a clear strategy.

7. Section Seven: 15 Minutes a Day for Financial Change

How to exploit15 minutes a day to improve your financial situation?

Improving your financial situation does not necessarily mean making big changes or investing in huge projects. Rather, tangible improvement can be achieved by using short periods of time each day in a smart and organized way. Allocating15 minutes a day may seem small, but if you invest that time effectively in improving your financial awareness and taking small, consistent steps, you may notice a big change in your financial situation over time. In this article, we will discuss how to use those few minutes productively.

1.Setting goalsFinanceDaily

Start by setting small, achievable daily goals.15 minutes. For example, you could start by assessing your daily expenses and determining if there is room for reduction. The goal here is to be realistic and set specific, measurable goals. For example:

- Review monthly bills and try to reduce them (subscriptions, electronic services).
- Set a specific amount to save daily or weekly.

This helps you develop the habit of constantly thinking about improving your financial situation rather than relying on sporadic or random initiatives.

2. Financial education

One of the best ways to improve your financial situation is to continually educate yourself about money, investing and saving.15 minutes a day to read financial articles, watch educational videos, or listen to a podcast about money and investing. You can, for example, dedicate time to this activity in the morning or evening.

- Learn the basics of investing in stocks and real estate.
- Explore expert tips on how to manage expenses and increase savings.
- Learn how to create a solid personal budget.

Financial education increases your awareness and enables you to make smarter financial decisions.

3. Expense analysis and gap identification

Take some time each day to analyze your personal expenses. Review your bank accounts and identify where money is being spent inefficiently. You may notice that you are spending unnecessary amounts on subscriptions or services that you do not benefit from. Once you identify these expenses, you can start reducing or eliminating them entirely.

- Record your daily expenses with a simple financial app.

- Compare your income and expenses and see if you need to adjust your budget.
- Find ways to redirect this money into investments or savings.

Constant tracking helps you control your spending and increases your chances of saving.

4. Improve negotiation skills

in15 minutes a day, you can improve your negotiation skills which will help you get better deals whether in your professional or personal life. Whether it is buying a product or negotiating a salary increase at work. This time can be used to:

- Read articles or books about negotiation strategies.
- Watch educational videos to develop negotiation skills.
- Analyze trades you've made in the past and determine if you can improve their results.

Good negotiation can save you a lot of money in the long run.

5. Debt organization and reduction

If you are in debt, 15 minutes a day can be the perfect opportunity to come up with a plan to pay off debt faster. Analyze the interest rate on your debts, and start paying off those with the highest rate. You can also explore options like refinancing debt with lower interest.

- Calculate the interest you pay each month and look for alternatives to reduce it.
- Contact lenders to negotiate better terms.
- Make a plan to pay off your debts in the medium and long term.

Reducing debt means saving more money for the future.

6. Find ways to increase income.

Relying on one source of income may not be enough to improve your financial situation. You can take advantage of the 15 minutes a day looking for opportunities to increase your income through side hustles or simple investments.

- Think about your hobbies and whether you can turn them into an additional source of income.

- Explore freelance or part-time work opportunities in areas that require your skills.

- Explore simple investment methods like mutual funds or bonds.

Increasing income doesn't have to be a complicated process, you can start with simple steps and then expand the opportunities over time.

7. Improve saving habits

Saving isn't something that comes naturally to everyone, but you can take advantage of it.15 minutes a day to create healthy saving habits. For example:

- Set a certain percentage of your income to be automatically transferred to a savings account.

- Set a long-term savings goal (such as buying a house or car).

- Use savings apps that analyze your expenses and set aside small amounts each day to save.

Being organized and committed to saving gives you a solid financial foundation that you can rely on in tough times.

8. Review investment strategies

If you are already investing, take advantage ofTaking 15 minutes a day to review your investments can be helpful. Make sure your investments are moving in the right direction and are in line with your long-term financial goals. This doesn't mean you need to change your investment strategy every day, but staying informed will make your decisions more accurate.

- Review the performance of the stocks or bonds you have invested in.

- Stay up to date with financial market news and how it impacts your investments.

- Research new opportunities in the market that may be right for you.

9. Contact a financial advisor

Contacting a qualified financial advisor may be a smart move to improve your financial situation.For 15 minutes a day, you can write down a list of questions or issues you would like to discuss with a professional financial advisor. When you meet with the advisor, you will be better prepared and will make the most of this time.

- Attend financial workshops or virtual seminars.
- Learn about new investment opportunities and the risks associated with them.
- Ask questions about the best ways to plan for retirement or long-term investing.

10. Avoid emotional expenses.

Emotional expenditures are those we make as a result of certain feelings, whether positive or negative. You can useTake 15 minutes a day to assess how your emotions affect your financial decisions. Try to distinguish between basic needs and recreational desires that may negatively impact your budget.

- Ask yourself before every purchase: "Do I really need this?"
- Write a list of things that enhance your well-being without spending money.
- Try practicing meditation or financial awareness to reduce emotional expenses.

Conclusion

It can lead to 15 minutes a day of financial planning and organized financial activities can dramatically improve your financial situation over time. The key is commitment and consistency, because small improvements accumulated over time can make a big impact on your financial life.

Practical examples and quick tips to improve your income in a short time

Improving your income in a short time requires thinking outside the box and taking advantage of the opportunities available in the labor market and investment. There are many methods that you can follow to increase your income quickly, whether you are looking for additional income in addition to your current job or want to start a small project alongside your work. In this article, we will review **Practical examples** and **Quick Tips** You can easily implement it to improve your income in a short time.

1. Freelance

Freelancing has become one of the most popular ways to boost your income in a short time. Thanks to the Internet, you can now offer your services to millions of people and businesses around the world. Whether you have skills in graphic design, programming, writing, translation, or marketing, you can get started today.

Practical examples:

- **Writing articles** If you are good at writing, you can work as a content editor or article writer on platforms like: Upwork or Fiverr.

- **Graphic design** If you have design skills, you can offer logo design services and marketing materials to individuals and businesses.

- **Social Media Management**: Managing social media accounts for companies that do not have internal teams for this task.

Quick Tips:

- Define your niche and find platforms that meet your needs.

- Be sure to provide samples of your previous work to increase your chances of getting projects.

- Invest in improving your profile on freelance platforms so that you appear professional and trustworthy.

2. Affiliate Marketing

Affiliate marketing is a business model where you can earn extra income by promoting other companies' products or services in exchange for a commission. If you have a blog or social media account with a good following, you can start affiliate marketing.

Practical examples:

- Promote technology products through affiliate links on Amazon.

- Promote software services such as web hosting platforms or email marketing tools.

- Partner with local or international companies to promote their products through reviews or social media posts.

Quick Tips:

- Choose products or services that match your audience's interests.

- Use tracking links (tracking links) to measure the effectiveness of your promotional campaigns.

- Don't be too promotional or you will lose the trust of your followers; provide content with honest advice.

3. Investing in stocks and securities

If you are looking for a way to supplement your income without having to do extra work directly, investing in stocks may be a good option. Investing in the financial markets may allow you to make quick profits by speculating on stocks or investing in successful companies.

Practical examples:

- **Investing in stocks**: Buy stocks in large, fast-growing technology companies.

- **Investing in index funds (ETFs)** It is an easy way for new investors to invest their money in a group of diversified stocks without having to track each stock individually.

- **Daily speculationDay Trading)** It can be a quick way to make profits, but it requires good market and risk knowledge.

Quick Tips:

- Make sure you learn the basics of investing before you start, and stay away from high-risk investments at first.

- Use beginner-oriented investing apps like:Robinhood or eToro.

- Start with small amounts and focus on learning and long-term investing to achieve financial stability.

4.Sell products online

Trading products online is one of the fastest ways to make extra income. You can start a small business on sites likeAmazon, eBay or Etsy to sell products you make or buy in bulk.

Practical examples:

- **Print on demand (Print on Demand**Design t-shirts, hats or mugs and sell them online without having to purchase inventory in advance.

- **Wholesale**:Buy wholesale products from sites like:Alibaba and then resell them online.

- **Selling handmade products**If you have handicraft skills, you can sell your products onEtsy.

Quick Tips:

- Focus on one product at first until you master the business and understand its market.

- Use social media to promote your products and increase awareness of your brand.

- Find good suppliers and set competitive prices to ensure a good profit.

5.Working as a consultant (Consulting

If you have professional experience in a particular field, you can provide consulting services to individuals or companies that need your expertise. Working as a consultant can bring you a good extra income in a short time, especially if you can provide effective solutions to specific problems.

Practical examples:

- **Small Business Consulting**: Helping entrepreneurs improve marketing strategies or operational processes.

- **IT Consulting**: Provide advice on how to improve the technical infrastructure of small businesses.

- **Financial Consulting**: Helping individuals or companies manage money and invest.

Quick Tips:

- Clearly define your area of expertise, whether it's business, marketing, technology, or finance.

- Create a simple website that showcases your past experience and customer reviews.

- Offer attractive offers to new customers to build a strong reputation at the beginning.

6.leasingPropertyorTools

If you have property or tools that you don't use regularly, you can rent them out to others and generate extra income without having to put in much effort.

Practical examples:

- **Rent rooms or houses** If you have an extra room in your home, you can rent it out through sites like:Airbnb.

- **Tools and equipment rental** You can rent photography equipment, electrical appliances, or even cars.

- **Renting workspaces** If you have unused office space, you can rent it out to individuals or small businesses.

Quick Tips:

- Ensure that adequate insurance is provided for the rental property.

- Use trusted rental platforms to maintain your rights and protect your property.

- Provide excellent customer service to get positive reviews and increase your tenants.

7. Online Education

If you have experience or teaching skills in a particular field, you can turn that knowledge into additional income by offering online lessons.

Practical examples:

- **Providing educational courses** You can create video courses on topics of your specialty and sell them on platforms like:Udemy or Coursera.

- **Online Personal Training** You can offer private lessons in areas such as math, languages, or technical skills.

- **Direct education (Live Tutoring)**: Providing live educational sessions through platforms such as: Zoom or Google Meet.

Quick Tips:

- Identify your target audience and start providing content that matches their needs.
- Use tools like: Canva or PowerPoint to create professional presentations.
- Invest in good camera and audio equipment to deliver high-quality content.

8. Turn your hobby into a source of income

Personal hobbies can be a great way to earn extra income. If you have a hobby like photography, drawing, or cooking, you can turn it into a business that generates income.

Practical examples:

- **Photography** You can sell your photos online on sites like:Shutterstock or Adobe Stock.

- **Cooking** If you are good at cooking, you can offer home catering services or cooking classes.

- **Handicrafts**: Sell your paintings or crafts online or at local markets.

Quick Tips:

- Share your work on social media to increase exposure.

- Find local events and fairs to participate in.

- Be prepared to offer additional services to your customers such as customizing orders.

Conclusion

Improving your income in a short time depends on exploiting your existing skills, looking for available opportunities, and working smart. Whether you choose to freelance, invest, or sell products online, the important thing is to take the first step and continue improving. The above tips and examples give you direct and actionable ways to generate additional income as soon as possible.

Continuous Change: How Do You Continue to Develop Yourself Financially?

Personal financial development is an ongoing process that requires dedication and continuous learning, especially in our rapidly changing modern world. Achieving financial success is not just about reaching a specific goal, but rather an ongoing process that requires constant review and adjustment of strategies. In this article, we will discuss how you can continue to **Develop yourself financially** And how to adapt to rapid changes to achieve sustainable financial growth in the long term.

1. Promote continuing financial education

One of the most important factors in improving your financial situation is continuous learning. As financial markets and technology evolve, financial education becomes essential to understand the options available and avoid financial risks.

Ways to continue financial education:

- **reading financial books** There are many books that provide valuable insights into how to manage money and invest. Books like "Rich Dad, Poor Dad" by Robert Kiyosaki or "The Intelligent Investor" by Benjamin Graham are excellent sources of learning.

- **Subscribe to training courses** You can take advantage of online courses on investing, personal financial management, or even how to create a comprehensive financial plan.

- **Follow financial news**: Follow popular financial sites such as: Bloomberg or CNBC can help you stay up to date on major economic events that may impact your investments and financial decisions.

- **Listen to the financial podcast** If you're looking for a fun and easy way to get financial advice, listen to a financial podcast while you drive or exercise.

2. Review financial goals regularly.

Achieving financial stability requires setting clear, measurable financial goals, but these goals may need to be adjusted over time. As your life progresses, your financial priorities and needs may change. Therefore, it is important to review your financial goals regularly.

How to review financial goals:

- **Progress evaluation**Review your financial performance every three to six months. Compare your original goals with the results you have achieved so far. This helps you identify gaps and work to improve them.

- **Adjust goals based on new circumstances.**If you get a new job or get a raise, you may need to adjust your financial goals such as increasing your savings or investments.

- **Setting short-term and long-term goals**It is important to have a variety of financial goals. Short-term goals might include paying off debt or building an emergency fund, while long-term goals might be related to retirement or buying a home.

3. Expense and Budget Management

Effectively managing your expenses is an essential step to ensuring that your financial situation continues to improve. Creating and sticking to a budget ensures that you spend money wisely and allocate it to important things like saving and investing.

Steps to manage expenses effectively:

- **Track expenses**: Start by recording all your expenses for a certain period of time, whether daily or weekly. This will help you understand where your money is going and identify areas where you can cut back.

- **Reduce unnecessary expenses** After analyzing your expenses, you will discover the areas where you spend more than you need to. These could be unused subscriptions, meals out, or unnecessary shopping.

- **Use of financial applications** There are many applications that help you track your expenses and manage your budget better, such as: Mint or YNAB (You Need A Budget).

- **Savings and investment planning**: Allocate a portion of your monthly income to saving and investing. Create a savings plan that emphasizes regular saving, and stick to it until you achieve your financial goals.

4. Develop financial negotiation skills

Negotiation is a powerful tool for improving your financial situation, whether it's at work or in your personal life. Learning how to negotiate a salary, loans, or even large purchases can save you thousands of dollars over time.

Tips for developing negotiation skills:

- **Salary negotiation** When applying for a new job or reviewing your current salary, don't be afraid to negotiate a higher salary. Research the average salaries in your field and use this information to support your application.

- **Negotiate prices**: If you are going to buy something expensive like a car or electronics, do not accept the first price you are offered. Always try to negotiate to get the best deal.

- **Negotiate financial benefits** If you are dealing with debt or loans, try negotiating with the bank to lower interest or refinance the debt at lower rates.

5. Continuous investment and diversification of investments

Investing is one of the best ways to build long-term financial wealth. However, it is important to learn how to diversify and adjust your investments over time to ensure you minimize risk and maximize returns.

Continuous investment strategies:

- **Regular investment**It is important to continue investing regularly, even if the amounts are small. This allows you to benefit from the price averaging strategy (Dollar-Cost Averaging), where you buy more assets when prices are low and less when prices are high.

- **Diversify the investment portfolio**: Don't put all your money in one type of asset like stocks or real estate. Instead, diversify your portfolio across different markets like bonds, cryptocurrencies, ETFs, and more.

- **Review investments regularly.**It is important to review your investment performance regularly, to ensure that your strategies are still in line with your financial goals. If some assets are not performing as you expected, you may need to adjust or change your strategy.

6. Flexibility in dealing with economic changes

The financial world is full of changes, whether they are caused by local or global economic developments. You must be able to adapt to these changes quickly and effectively to avoid potential financial risks.

How to adapt to economic changes:

- **Periodic market analysis**: Stay up to date with the movements of the financial and economic markets. This will enable you to make informed investment decisions based on current conditions.

- **Preparing for financial emergencies** Build an emergency fund with enough money to cover your expenses for a period of 3 to 6 months. This will give you financial security if you face any economic disruptions such as job loss or a recession.

- **Diversify sources of income** It is good to have more than one source of income, whether it is through a side job or multiple investments. This reduces your dependence on one source of income and increases your financial stability.

7. Invest time in learning new skills.

The modern economy is constantly evolving, and skills that were valuable ten years ago may not be so today. Investing your time in learning new skills can help boost your financial prospects in the long run.

How to develop new skills:

- **Continuous learning**: Identify the skills you need to develop to increase your chances in the job market or to start a business. For example, you may need to learn programming, digital marketing, or data analysis.

- **Join training courses** There are many educational platforms such as:Coursera, Udemy, and LinkedIn Learning offer courses in various fields.

- **Connect with experts**: Benefit from the expertise of others by joining business networking groups or connecting with experts in your field. This may help you discover new opportunities or improve your current strategies.

8. Planning for retirement properly

Retirement planning is not something that should be left for last, but should be part of your financial development strategy from the very beginning of your working life. Failure to plan well for retirement can lead to significant financial stress in the future.

Retirement planning steps:

- **Start saving early**The earlier you start saving for retirement, the better your chances of building a strong retirement fund. Use tax-advantaged retirement accounts such as**Individual Retirement Accounts (IRAs)IRA)**or**Plans401(k)**To provide tax benefits that help you boost your savings. Invest a portion of your monthly income on a regular basis in these accounts to maximize compound interest.

- **Setting retirement goals**Before you start saving for retirement, determine what your future needs are. Think about how you want to live after retirement, and where you want to live. This will help you determine how much money you need to build a sustainable retirement fund.

- **Investing Wisely for Retirement**: While saving for retirement, it is important to invest wisely to ensure sustainable growth. Choose low-cost investments such as index funds (ETFs) that track the performance of major markets. This tool provides you with good diversification at a lower cost, which helps reduce risk and achieve good returns in the long run.

- **Review and adjust retirement plans regularly.** As your life progresses and your financial circumstances change, you may need to adjust your retirement plans. Review your plan every few years to ensure it aligns with your current goals and circumstances, whether that means adjusting your savings level or changing your investment strategies.

9. Prepare for financial risks

Sustainable financial development requires planning for potential risks. Whether these risks come from economic crises, health emergencies, or changes in the labor market, being able to deal with these risks proactively protects your financial position and increases your chances of success.

How to prepare for financial risks:

- **Building an emergency fund** As mentioned earlier, an emergency fund is essential to any financial plan. It is best to have an amount equivalent to your living expenses for a period of 3 to 6 months to cover unexpected crises such as job loss or emergency medical expenses.

- **Getting the right insurance** Insurance is an important tool in protecting against financial risks. Make sure you are covered by health insurance, life insurance, and property insurance such as car and home insurance. Good insurance can protect you from unexpected large bills that could significantly impact your financial situation.

- **Legal Planning** You should have a legal plan to protect your assets and secure your legacy. Preparing a will and updating it regularly ensures that your money and property are distributed as you wish after you are gone. Effective tax planning also helps you minimize any taxes that may be imposed on your estate.

10. Flexibility and patience

It is important to be flexible when dealing with finances, as markets and economies are constantly changing. You must be prepared to adapt to these changes, whether they are positive or negative. Sometimes, you may experience financial setbacks, but the key here is patience and flexibility in re-evaluating your goals and strategies.

How to be flexible in developing yourself financially:

- **Adapting to economic changes** Economic crises or epidemics such as the COVID-19 pandemic may lead to:COVID-19 has brought significant changes to the job market and investments. You need to be prepared to adjust your financial plans based on new circumstances. For example, you may need to increase your savings during a recession or look for investment opportunities in promising new sectors.

- **Avoid rash decisions.**: Sometimes, financial pressures can lead you to make rash decisions like selling investments at the wrong time or jumping into ill-considered opportunities. Being patient and sticking to long-term strategies can help you overcome challenges.

Conclusion

Continuous financial development requires a combination of self-education, wise spending management, sustainable investing, and flexibility and patience. By adopting sound financial habits such as setting clear goals, reviewing your finances regularly, and preparing for economic changes, you can build strong and sustainable financial stability.

With these tips, you will be able to balance hard work with financial intelligence to ensure long-term financial growth. Most importantly, remember that the process requires patience and discipline, and that financial progress comes gradually with time and dedication.

15 Minutes a Day to Financial Transformation: The John Paul DeJoria Story

In the world of business, there are many people who did not start out rich, but managed to achieve great success through dedication and perseverance. Among these people is John Paul DeJoria, a man who succeeded in overcoming all economic and social challenges to become one of the most prominent businessmen in the United States of America. John Paul's story begins in poverty and deprivation, but it tells the story of how daily commitment and the search for small opportunities can change the course of a person's life.

Humble beginnings

John Paul DeJoria was born inApril 13, 1944 in Los Angeles, California. His family was of Italian and Greek descent, and their financial circumstances were not at all comfortable. When he was two years old, his parents separated, which increased the financial burden on his mother who struggled to provide a decent life for her children. From here, the features of DeJoria's life began to take shape, as he learned from a young age the meaning of struggle and patience.

At the age of ten, John Paul DeJoria started his first job selling newspapers on the street to help make ends meet for his family. Despite his young age, this experience was the beginning of his financial awareness and the development of his money skills. He realized that life requires more than just waiting for opportunities, it must be created. These were the first lessons on his path to success.

The road to success is full of difficulties

After graduating from high school, John Paul joined the US Navy to gain some skills and experience. But after his discharge, he found himself facing life alone. He was facing a real crisis as he was homeless for a period of time, and lived in his car for several months. This period was one of the most difficult moments of his life, as he had very little money, and he had to decide whether to give up or look for an opportunity to change his reality.

But what set DeJoria apart was his refusal to give up. He believed that life held many opportunities, and that he could change the course of his life if he committed to changing his daily behavior and way of thinking. He began looking for small opportunities that could open the doors to success. And that's when the idea of starting a hair care company came to him.

Paul Mitchell Company Founded

In the year 1980, after years of moving between odd jobs and trying to break into the business world, John Paul and his friend Paul Mitchell raised just $700 to start their own hair care company. The beginning was very humble, as they worked out of a small apartment and marketed the products themselves. At the time, they did not have a huge budget for advertising or big marketing campaigns. It was all about personal relationships and determination to succeed.

John Paul was spending 15 minutes a day to organize his thoughts and make short-term plans to increase sales and expand their business. He took every opportunity to develop himself and his company, and soon Paul Mitchell's hair care products began to attract attention and achieve great success. By committing this short time daily, DeJoria was able to direct the course of his business in an intelligent and focused manner.

The role of the 15 minutes daily

What made John Paul DeJoria successful was his reliance on a simple but highly effective strategy: a commitment to allocating 15 minutes a day to think about improving his financial situation and developing his business. This period of time may seem short, but it was the key to his success. He spent this time reviewing his financial goals, analyzing ways to improve the business, and thinking about innovation. Those few minutes gave him the clarity and direction he needed to achieve long-term success.

One of DeJoria's greatest pieces of advice for those seeking financial success was to start small and consistent. He realized that success does not happen overnight, but is the cumulative result of small daily efforts directed toward a goal. And this was theThe daily 15 minutes were an investment in himself and his work, resulting in his personal and professional growth.

From poverty to billions

Over time, Paul Mitchell grew tremendously, becoming one of the most popular brands in the hair care world. As a result of this success, John Paul DeJoria's fortune reached billions of dollars. However, financial success was not the only aspect that distinguished DeJoria. He became an inspirational figure for many who believe that difficult beginnings mean that success is impossible.

Today, John Paul DeJoria owns several businesses and projects, including:Patrón Spirits, a premium spirits company, has significantly increased his wealth. Despite his enormous wealth, John Paul DeJoria has not forgotten his humble roots. On the contrary, he uses his wealth to support several charitable causes and humanitarian initiatives. He has learned through personal experience that true success is not limited to accumulating wealth, but also how to use that wealth to change the lives of others.

Lessons learned

The story of John Paul DeJoria offers several valuable lessons for people seeking to improve their financial situation and change their lives. First, the story emphasizes that success does not necessarily require perfect beginnings. Anyone can achieve their goals if they are willing to work hard and be dedicated. Second, it shows the importance of consistency and sustainable thinking. Customization15 minutes a day for financial planning or developing a project can have a huge impact in the long run.

Finally, the story of John Paul DeJoria offers a lesson in the importance of self-belief. Despite all the challenges he faced early in his life, he never lost faith in his abilities or the potential for success. This self-belief was one of the main factors that helped him overcome obstacles and achieve his dreams.

Conclusion

John Paul DeJoria's story is a living testament that financial success is not limited to the rich or the privileged. Anyone, regardless of their circumstances, can make a dramatic difference in their life through hard work and small but consistent steps. The key is to use every day, no matter how short, to improve yourself and strive for the best.

It's not about the length of time, it's about consistency and focus on goals.

End of the book:15 minutes change your life

Success is not a destination at the end of the road, but rather an ongoing journey filled with challenges and situations that we face every day. If there is one lesson you can take from this book, it is that success does not come all at once or as a result of one decision, but rather is the result of a series of small decisions that we make every day, those decisions that may seem simple but contribute greatly to achieving our goals.

We have seen how15 minutes a day can change someone's life like John **Paul DeJoria** From poverty and homelessness to building a business empire. Those daily minutes were the key that opened the doors of success for him. In the end, there is no magic or big secret behind success. It is about commitment, perseverance and hard work every day.

The importance of time and planning

For each of us24 hours in a day, but how we use those hours is what makes the difference between successful people and the rest. Taking 15 minutes a day to think and plan, to improve yourself, or to learn something new can have a huge impact on your life. It may not seem like much time, but it's enough to make a positive difference if used wisely.

Imagine you are spending 15 minutes a day learning a new skill or improving one you already have. After a month, you'll have spent 7.5 hours on the activity, and after a year, you'll have over 90 hours of improvement and learning. These numbers show how small, consistent efforts can have a huge impact. They're like drops of water hitting a rock, and over time, those drops can make a big dent.

Commitment and dedication

Success is not achieved without commitment. The person who is committed to developing himself and his ideas every day is the person who will ultimately achieve success. It is not the person who has the most money or the best resources, but the person who can use his time effectively. Your commitment to allocate 15 minutes a day to improve your financial or personal situation is the first step towards achieving your big goals.

Dedication is another equally important element. You may face many challenges along the way, but if you are committed to change and development, you will always find a way to overcome those challenges. You will find that there is always an opportunity in every difficult situation, and that every challenge is a lesson that adds to your experiences and makes you stronger.

Belief in the ability to change

If you believe you can make a difference, you will see opportunities that others may miss. Self-confidence is a key ingredient to success. If you believe you can, you will find the means to make it happen. This is what sets successful people apart. They don't wait for perfect circumstances; they create the circumstances that help them succeed.

If you spend 15 minutes a day improving yourself or working toward your goals, you build a strong foundation for success. You may not notice results right away, but over time you will start to see small improvements that add up into big accomplishments.

Consistency is key.

If there is one final piece of advice to be given, it is this:Contentiousness doesn't come to those who work hard for one day and then quit, it comes to those who commit themselves to a path of continuous improvement. It's the small changes you make every day that contribute to building a better life and a brighter future.

So, don't underestimate the power of the15 minutes. Start your day by setting a simple goal and work towards it, even if it means dedicating a small amount of time at first. Over time, you will start to see the results and the difference these small habits can make.

Ultimately, success is not limited to the rich or the lucky. It is available to anyone who has the desire to improve and the commitment. All you need is the will to change and the time each day to dedicate to achieving your goals.

a summary

Each of us has the power to change our lives. All it takes is making the decision to set aside time each day to develop and work hard. The beginning may not be perfect, and you may face difficulties, but the commitment to continuous progress is what will ultimately lead you to success. **15 minutes daily-It** may seem like a small amount of time, but it could be the factor that changes your life completely.

Don't wait for tomorrow. Start today. Take15 minutes, and start changing your life.